You Better Not Cry

ALSO BY AUGUSTEN BURROUGHS

You Better Not Cry

True Stories for Christmas

AUGUSTEN
BURROUGHS

Atlantic Books
LONDON

First published in the United States of America in 2009 by
St. Martin's Press, 175 Fifth Avenue, New York, N.Y. 10010.

First published in hardback and export and airside
trade paperback in Great Britain in 2009 by Atlantic Books,
an imprint of Grove Atlantic Ltd.

Every effort has been made to trace or contact all copyright holders.
The publishers will be pleased to make good any omissions or rectify
any mistakes brought to their attention at the earliest opportunity.

Hardback ISBN: 978 184887 246 2
Export and airside trade paperback ISBN: 978 184887 320 9

Book design by Phil Mazzone

1 3 5 7 9 10 8 6 4 2

Printed in Great Britain by the MPG Books Group

Atlantic Books
An imprint of Grove Atlantic Ltd
Ormond House
26–27 Boswell Street
London
WC1N 3JZ

www.atlantic-books.co.uk

The names and identifying characteristics of some people have been changed.

This book is dedicated to the people of Australia who lost everything there is to lose in the February fires of 2009.

And to everyone who still holds their breath to listen for the sound of distant sleigh bells in the sky.

Author's Note

This book was written on a Linux-powered computer using open-source software that is available to everyone, free.

Contents

Acknowledgments

I am grateful to my friends and family, publishers and management, both here in the United States and abroad. Most of all, I am grateful to my readers, who have made me feel so less alone in the world.

I stopped believing in Santa Claus when I was six. Mother took me to see him in a department store, and he asked for my autograph.

—Shirley Temple

You Better Not Cry

You Better Not Cry

*I*T'S NOT THAT I was an outright nitwit of a child. It's that the things even a nitwit could do with little or no instruction often confused me. Simple, everyday sorts of things tripped me up.

Stacking metal chairs, for example. Everybody in class just *seemed to know* exactly how to fold the seat up into the back and then nest them all together like Pringles potato chips. I sat on the floor for ten minutes with one of the things as if somebody had told me to just stare at it. *Concentrate hard, Augusten, try and turn it into an eggplant with your mind. You can do it!*

The other children appeared to be born with some sort of innate knowledge, as though the action of folding and stacking child-size metal school chairs was genetically encoded within each of them, like finger-nails or a sigmoid colon.

I seemed to lack the ability to comprehend the obvious. From the very beginning there had been warning signs.

Like every kid just starting school, I had to memorize the Pledge of Allegiance—something that would in many towns today be considered *prayer* and therefore forbidden; akin to forcing a child to drink the blood of a sacrificial goat or unfurl a Tabriz prayer rug and kneel barefoot on it while facing Mecca.

While I managed to learn the words, memorizing isn't the same as *understanding*. And of course I was never tested on the meaning of the pledge. It must have simply been taken for granted that even the dimmest child would easily grasp the meaning of a phrase such as *I pledge allegiance,* especially when that phrase was spoken while standing at strict attention and facing the American flag, hand in a salute above the heart. There was so little room for misinterpretation. It was the Pledge of Allegiance, not *Are You There God? It's Me, Margaret.*

Still. If one of the teachers had asked me to explain the meaning of those words—which I chanted parrot-minded and smiling each morning—they certainly would have been shocked to hear me admit that while I didn't know *exactly* what it was about, I knew it had something to do with Pledge, the same furniture polish my mother used and that always, inexplicably, made me feel sunny. So each morning as I spoke those hallowed words, it was the bright yellow can with the glowing lemony scent that I pictured.

It was another, more profound misunderstanding that caused so much trouble.

As a young child I had Santa and Jesus all mixed up. I could identify Coke or Pepsi with just one sip, but I could not tell you for sure why they strapped Santa to a cross. Had he missed a house? Had a good little girl somewhere in the world not received the doll he'd promised her, making the father angry?

My confusion may have stemmed from the fact that I was being raised without religion, except for a brief and entirely baffling period of Sunday school. But I certainly never detected any theological undertones in my Sunday school sessions. Mostly it was just a dank, gloomy day spent in the basement of the Unitarian Church where we were expected to play with old-time toys made out of metal; little figures like a nurse in a white uniform, a policeman, a child, a mother holding a skillet. The rest of the world had long ago moved on to plastic *action figures*; the newest ones with articulating arms and legs. Many were even holding guns. What kind of crazy school made kids spend the day in a basement and play with some dumb nurse with a little cap like they only wore on black-and-white *Leave It to Beaver*? About the only thing you could do with these old things was pick away the lead paint and nibble the flecks—tiny crunch, salty.

They didn't even have real teachers, just a bunch of ladies that were old and papery and drank all our apple juice.

While I'd heard the words, *Christian, Catholic,* and *Jewish* I never connected them to Santa or Jesus. I assumed they were geographical terms, like *Canadian* or *Military.*

Everything I knew of God and Jesus—along with Santa, for that matter—I knew from television.

And this just confused the issue further. Because both Santa and Jesus appeared in continuous rotation on television at the same time each year—and both of them were pushing Christmas.

Just after Thanksgiving it would begin: the parade of holiday specials. There was *Rudolph the Red-Nosed Reindeer* and *Davey and Goliath*'s "Christmas Lost & Found," where they lived in what appeared to be a corrugated-steel storage unit. I loved dogs, but I despised that preachy, do-gooder of a cur, Goliath—always Davey's killjoy.

"C'mon, Goliath, let's go grab a little girl by her ponytail and make her eat yellow snow."

"Gee, Day-vee, I'm not sure we should be doing that. That doesn't sound sanitary. And cleanliness Day-vee, is next to godliness."

I swear. If I were Davey, I would have fed that thing a bowl of warm mayonnaise and nails.

After *Davey and Goliath* it was on to *The Grinch* or *Charlie Brown,* before moving along to *The Three Wise Men.* It was a jumble of mixed messages: One minute, I was told the "magic" of Christmas was a jolly man in a red suit, slinging a sack filled with packages over his shoulder. And the next, it was drilled into my head that the real "meaning" of Christmas was Jesus, just a little baby on a stack of wheat. Then they would show him as a grown-up hippie dressed in a skimpy little outfit like the one Ginger wore on *Gilligan's Island.* He walked around casting spells on kids with harelips and other deformities, and making cripples magically rise from their wheelchairs—which I assumed he had given to them for Christmas in the first place.

So while it was Santa during prime time, those shadowy, almost-but-not-quite hours before were often given to Jesus.

But in both, December twenty-fifth was the big day. Even I knew that much.

What I didn't know was why you might see Jesus in front of one house—even a whole barn scene with the wheat and everything—but then the next house might have a sleigh and reindeer and then Santa himself on the roof. Or sometimes, somebody would have it all: Jesus on the wheat, Santa on his sleigh, and even Frosty, waving at the traffic and starting to melt. They always showed him starting to melt.

Frosty made me sad because everybody knew that he was going to die. That in and of itself was confusing, because why hadn't Jesus visited him and used a spell? Jesus could have turned Frosty into a block of ice for all of eternity, if he wanted to.

The music of the season further added to my confusion. How was I supposed to tell Santa and Jesus apart when we sang, "He knows when you've been bad or good," when it was Jesus who watched you all the time? And then when we had to sing, "Oh, come let us adore him," which one did they mean? I figured Santa, because it was on his lap we were allowed to sit. I imagined you'd probably get in trouble if you tried to sit on Jesus. From what I'd seen on TV, Jesus could touch *you* pretty much anywhere he wanted but you could get turned into a hedgehog if you touched him. My mother had a friend like that, one you couldn't touch. She wasn't able to turn you into a hedgehog or anything, but she would shriek if you bumped her elbow by accident, and even if you said you were sorry, you could see her trying with her eyes to turn you into something.

So I wondered, was Santa Jesus's father? That made sense to me except for the confusing matter with the Three Wise Men and Joseph.

My understanding was that back in the olden-days before electricity and Santa, they made old bums hand out the presents. But in those days they had only junk to give—stinky incense, sticks, and little bits of camel-tail yarn. I figured these were the kinds of presents Jesus probably gave the cripples today. Gifts that the regular children, like myself, wouldn't want or even notice were missing, but that the cripples would be thrilled to receive and could weave into pot holders.

Then they had to go and throw Joseph at me. Who the hell was Joseph?

It turned out, he was Mary's husband, so that made him the father of Jesus. But I had been under the impression that *God* was Jesus's father. So was Joseph God? Was Joseph also Santa?

When Joseph just kind of vanished, I figured he was probably in the basement drinking, just like my own father.

7

Sometimes, I would stand at my window at two in the morning and wave into the dark. "Come get me, Jesus, take me back up there with you to the toy farm," I would whisper, making sure my lips were easy to read.

Despite all my confusion I managed to make two distinctions: *Santa* was the one who climbed around on peoples' roofs then entered their private homes at night as they slept, while *Jesus* was the one that made surprise visits—mostly to crippled kids and people who were crying. I thought they both might wear a red suit from time to time.

At night when I prayed to Jesus, it was a jolly man in a red suit—with access to the world's supply of presents—whom I imagined listening to my prayers and taking notes. And when I was afraid or needed serious assistance, I prayed to the skinny hippie Jesus coming down from the North Pole in maybe a VW Bus or on a broom where he could wave his hand over my head and make the problem go away.

When the Abominable Snowman had cornered Rudolph in the glittering ice cave, I watched in rapt silence. "Jesus, where are you? *Help them!* Get a gun, Jesus, get a gun!"

One sorry December my confusion reached a kind of tipping point and resulted in a brief hospitalization.

My grandparents, gruff Jack and glamorous Carolyn, were driving up north from Lawrenceville, Georgia, to spend Christmas with us. They owned a silver Cadillac Fleetwood with bloodred leather seats. The interior of that car smelled so wonderful that when I went down south to visit them in the summer, I'd spend the first hour sitting in the back of the car in the driveway, sniffing the rarefied air: cigarettes, my grandmother's Guerlain perfume, butterscotch hard candies, Lavoris mouthwash, and the seat leather all resting atop a hushed, gamey base note of mink.

I loved mink. I would have worn it if allowed. In fact, I would have enjoyed a mink version of my one-piece hooded pajama set with attached feet. The idea of being covered in mink head-to-toe was thrilling.

My brother said mink was "a waste of perfectly good predators needed to keep the vole, shrew, mouse, and frog populations at reasonable levels." He said they should make coats out of house cats instead. "Cats are plentiful," were his exact words. The idea of wearing a tabby cat coat was also appealing. But mink reminded me of my grandmother, so I still loved it most.

All week it had been physically painful to wait for my grandparents' arrival. It was impossible not to ask when they were coming, just like it was impossible not to look down the street in the direction of the bus when you were waiting for it. I had tried looking in the opposite direction but it itched my brain to an unbearable degree.

"How many more days now?" I whined to my mother, clutching at my stomach, which was distended with cheese popcorn.

She whined right back at me. "*Please* stop asking me that question, it's only been an hour since you last asked and the answer has not changed. *They will be here in six more days.* And for God's sake, stop licking my matches— *put those down right now*—they won't strike if they're wet."

I pictured, with a sinking, bottomless feeling in my chest, the moon. There would be one tonight. It was *hours and hours* away from appearing; only *after* all the sun had finally burned out and rolled away to the far side of the sky where we couldn't see it; only after the sky itself bruised pink and violet-black would the moon show up. And then it wouldn't do anything but hang there like a stop sign to all the people on Earth who could see it. And I would have to wait for *six* moons to come and go. *Almost ten of them.* "They might as well never come," I said, miserably.

"They will be here before you know it, you'll see,"

my mother said. Then she announced that she was opening a can of smoked oysters and would I like one?

"Are there any pearls in there?"

"I haven't found one yet," she said.

"Then, no."

"But you remember what I told you about your
granddaddy, my father, right?"

I glared at her. I hated when she talked about him
because she made him seem so nice, like the best grandfather of all, and he was dead and had always been
dead except when I was a baby and he held me, which
didn't count because I couldn't remember. It was like
she was holding out a candy bar before dropping it into
the toilet.

"Remember how I told you he found a pearl in a can
of oysters once?"

I remembered. After I opened the twenty-four cans
of oysters my mother had purchased on sale at Stop &
Shop, looking for pearls, she yelled at me for so many
days it would have been impossible to forget. "Yeah, he
found a pearl. But it was broken," I said.

"It wasn't broken," she corrected. "It had been
cooked. Along with the oysters in the can. But I still
thought it was just the most magical thing I had ever
seen. A pearl, right there in a can of oysters."

I once thought I found a piece of scrap metal inside a Hostess cupcake but that wasn't the same.

"Okay, now how long before they get here?" I asked.

Six moons later I was standing in the kitchen about to eat a breakfast of fresh cake batter when the doorbell rang. It was as if I were a lab rat and had received an electric shock. My body jerked, causing the wooden mixing spoon in my hand to sway violently off course and I ended up with raw cake batter all over my nose and chin, glops of it splattered down the front of my shirt. I tossed the spoon onto the kitchen counter, wiped a pot holder across my face, threw it onto the stovetop, and ran from the room.

When I opened the front door, my grandparents, Jack and Carolyn, were standing there on the landing, their arms linked. Beside my grandfather stood Jesus himself. He was almost as tall as my grandfather and he was dressed in his full regalia: red suit with white fur trim, black glossy boots. I could barely take it all in, let alone contain myself. If I had known the word for what had just descended, I certainly would have used it:

the Rapture. I shrieked hysterically, *"Jesus! It's Jesus! Jeeeeeeeeee-*zus!"

My mother had joined me at the front door and was about to open her mouth in greeting when I screamed. My grandmother flinched and her smile evaporated. My grandfather winced and covered his left ear, the one closest to my trap. *"What* the hell? Somebody knock that boy alongside the head," he bellowed over my din.

My grandmother was distressed. She leaned forward and spoke over my shouts. "What are you saying about Jesus, honey?" Even when her voice was raised, her rich, melodic Southern accent made everything she said seem like ice cream scooped from a container—sweet, with gently rolled edges.

I stabbed my index finger at the life-size plush toy. "It's Jesus!"

My grandmother stepped forward and lowered herself so that she was nearly at eye level with me. She smiled kindly. "This isn't Jesus, sugar, it's *Santa,* you see? He has a red suit and everything." She turned her head and glanced over her shoulder at the stuffed Santa still standing beside her husband in the doorway. Then she looked back at me.

"It's a sin to call Santa *Jesus.* *'Thou shalt have no other gods before thee.'* That's from the King James Bible, honey.

Don't you read your King James, a big boy like you, eight years old? Aren't you doing well in your Bible study classes?"

For a fleeting instant, she had captured my attention. *"King?"* I said, picturing a diamond the size of a ham bone.

My mother said, "He doesn't attend Bible study, Carolyn." But she was taking so much Mellaril that when she spoke, it sounded like her tongue had swollen to the size of a hog's and also like she'd been drinking since the day before yesterday. "And I am tho thorry for hith outburtht, pleath come in." She motioned with her trembling arm, extending her unsteady welcome into the house.

As my grandparents walked guardedly past her, my grandfather hoisting Santa/Jesus around the waist and carrying him into the house sideways, it seemed my mother might fall over. Her face was frozen into an unfamiliar expression of almost plastic contentedness and calm, a small tight smile locked onto her lips. But I could see the panic in her eyes. She looked as if she had been hijacked by her face and was now trapped forever inside a pleasant, ordinary woman. She leaned her shoulder against the wall. "Woo you like a thuna samwhich?" she muttered, seemingly unaware that it was

14

just after eight in the morning. I just stared at her and rolled my eyes.

My mother's psychiatrist always had her on one pill or another. Sometimes, the effects could be quite entertaining. I liked best the pills that made her sleep. For days. It gave me the opportunity to paint her eyelids with blue chalk dust and apply a wide coating of lipstick, doubling the size of her lips. I saw my sleeping, made-up mother not as clownish but as beautiful.

Inspired by the "earthy" new generation of women like Carole King, who wore no makeup and looked like a farmhand, my mother had stopped wearing anything on her face. *Maybe* she would wear lip-colored lipstick, which only made her look as if she had just eaten a greasy drumstick and not wiped her mouth.

My mother pulled herself together and followed after my grandparents in her side-effect shuffle, wiping her hands on the hips of her black slacks. I noticed that her black turtleneck was on inside out, the white tag making her look like something that could still be returned to the store.

My grandfather was now standing in the center of the kitchen, turning around and around, Jesus/Santa still under his arm.

First, Santa's head knocked against my cake batter

bowl and sent it skittering to the edge of the counter, where my grandmother swooped forward and caught it just in time. Then Jesus's glossy black boots smacked my grandmother in the back of her head as Jesus/Santa came around again. "Jesus, Santa old boy, I'd hate to see you after a few highballs!" my grandfather chuckled.

And I thought, *My* grandfather *calls him Jesus/Santa,* too. Now I was desperately confused.

"Damn it, Jack, stand in one place or you'll destroy the whole kitchen!" my grandmother shouted, her hands fluttering around the back of her head, repairing her hairstyle.

"Aw, hell," my grandfather finally said, "let's set this ol' boy down in the living room next to the tree." And with that, he turned one last time and walked back out through the kitchen doorway, Carolyn scurrying after him with her arms already outstretched, ready to catch whatever it was that came crashing down.

Her internal clock obviously unwound, my mother commented, "Why, I've never *seen* such a thing. He's nearly life-size. He sure does take over the kitchen!"

In a mean little voice I whispered, *"They've already left the room."*

But Jack had heard her with his basset hound ears. "He sure as hell does. And let me tell you, we had a hell of a time fitting the old boy in the car, but we finally just lay him on his side in the backseat and Carolyn here gave him a good shove and we shut the door. Made it up here in record time, too."

When I stepped into the living room I couldn't even breathe. He'd set Jesus/Santa down right beside the tree and it was an overwhelming sight. *Here he was, all for me.*

I felt overjoyed, like one of the crippled wheelchair kids on TV when Jesus floats down and shines his light on them.

This year, our tree was so tall it nearly touched the central cedar beam of the cathedral ceiling. It was the tallest tree we'd ever had and my father almost didn't get it. He was worried it wouldn't fit on top of the car; then he was worried it wouldn't fit inside the house. He threatened to get this stumpy, awful little tree that looked like an angry fat person, all crooked and lopsided. It reminded me of my mother before she went on Weight Watchers. When I mentioned this to my father—"Doesn't it remind you of her? Especially from the side?"—he immediately turned away from the angry stump tree and said, "We'll get the other one."

I stepped forward and looked up at the glorious tree and my Jesus/Santa standing guard beside it.

Now, the garbage my mother had added to the tree

no longer bothered me. It was as if Jesus/Santa had made all of her trash simply *vanish*.

My mother placed her own "fragile and very special" ornaments on the top half of the tree, out of my reach. *Where I couldn't smash them,* I knew she was thinking. But she flattered herself; I had no interest in her beige angels made from common barn straw or her Three Wise Men crafted entirely from Indian corn. And if she thought I had any interest in her precious little walnut-shell mouse, she truly was crazy and should be locked away.

Blech.

Why would anybody pollute a Christmas tree with such filth? Why stop at corncobs and straw and nutshells; why not just glue dirt and puff balls to the branches?

A Christmas tree should be wrapped around and around and around with a dazzling gold garland. And then tinsel should cling to every branch—in clumps, not stingy *strands*. And there should be lights, dozens of them. All blinking. And then gold and silver balls, some coated with sparkly glitter, the others with tiny mirrors. And maybe it would be okay to have a few other things, as long as they were either illuminated or gold-electroplated.

I noticed that even in the wide-open, breathy light

of the morning that diffused the living room, I could see the bright red, green, blue, yellow, orange, and white lights from the tree reflected in Jesus/Santa's shiny black boots.

I wanted those boots.

On Jesus/Santa's face—so true to life—was an expression of genuine affection.

I wanted that face.

My grandfather had led my grandmother and mother into the kitchen. I heard the freezer door open then the shattering smack of a bag of ice hitting the counter. In an instant, my father came ambling up the stairs. The ice had called him like a dog whistle: *Special occasion cocktails in the morning!*

I heard my grandfather's sonic boom. "Well, hey there old man! How are ya, boy? Where the hell have you been? Your mama and I have been here for hours already."

I just couldn't believe it. This was, *this was* . . . I didn't have the words to even describe the euphoria I felt. Not only would I love having Santa right here in the house with us for Christmas, but when the holidays were over, I would move Jesus right into my bedroom and he would live with me, full time.

My mother stuck her sweaty head out the kitchen doorway. "Augusten," she called, "you can play with Santa later, come on in here now with your grandparents and say hello."

"Coming," I shouted back. Then I quickly reached forward and touched the Jesus/Santa's crotch.

When I walked innocently into the kitchen, my grandmother clapped her hands together then patted her thighs. "Come here, precious, and sit on my lap."

I was still technically small enough to be able to fit on a lap. But in a matter of months, I would be banned from laps as I would shoot up almost a whole foot and weigh nearly as much as a big dog.

"Now, what's this business about referring to Santa as," and she whispered the name, "Jesus?"

I just looked at her and blinked.

"You know it's wrong for you to make fun of Jesus, don't you?"

I bristled at the mere suggestion, felt my small ears grow warm. I certainly *did* know this and furthermore, I wasn't making fun. "I know that," I said. "I would never say anything hateful about Jesus. That's why I'm so happy he's here."

My grandmother studied me, her thin, lined lips

puckering around a cigarette that wasn't there. "Now, honey, when you say you're so happy he's 'here,' you mean *here*, don't you?" and she placed her hand on her blouse, above her heart.

"*No*, Carolyn," I said, calling her by her first name as all the grandchildren did. "I mean, I'm glad he's here, in the house, out there in the living room next to the tree where Jack stuck him. You saw, you were there."

My grandmother was now flustered. "Jack," she said, "give me that," and she nodded to the drink in his hand. She meant business, so he took a step over and passed it to her. She grabbed the glass from his hand and took a deep swallow, then handed it back.

That's when she asked me, "Honey? Do you really think that big, red stuffed Santa we brought you is Jesus Christ, our Lord and Savior?"

The room fell eerily silent all of a sudden and everybody stared at me, waiting for my answer. It was the silliest question in the world, the answer so obvious that I was alerted to a possible trick.

I craned my neck around to look at my father, my mother, Jack—all of whom were looking at me expectantly.

"*Well,*" I said carefully, as though taking my first step across a frozen pond, listening for the crack of ice, "I know that he's *Santa*."

And my grandmother smiled, pleased with my answer, and patted me on the head.

"But he's *also* Jesus," I added. And I felt her stiffen beneath my legs.

"Margaret," Carolyn said, glowering at my mother, "what does he mean?"

My mother stepped over to the sink and ran the faucet over her cigarette, tossed it into the trash and immediately lit another. "I'm not sure what he means at all, Carolyn," she replied, the new calm smile still attached to her face. "Augusten, why do you say Jesus and Santa are the same? How so?"

So this is how it came to pass that I got my first lesson in Christian theology. Front row center on my grandmother's lap, I learned that what I had believed all my life was not only terribly wrong but deeply sinful and disrespectful.

In fact, I could likely burn in hell for all of eternity for my error.

Jesus was real. Jesus was God's own child, as surely as I was my mother's. He lived in the sky—not, *absurdly,* at the North Pole above *Canada*—and he invented everything, including Eskimos and goats.

"And Pop-Tarts?" I asked.

"No," my grandmother replied, "not Pop-Tarts."

She continued with the lesson. Jesus was the *Holy Father,* or at least his son.

"Which?" I asked.

"I told you," she said. "Jesus is our Lord and Savior."

"Then who's God?" I asked.

"Jesus is God," she replied.

"But you said Jesus was the son of God just as surely as I am the son of my mother."

My mother cleared her throat and everybody turned to face her. She asked, "I can't interest anybody in thum cheethe and crackerth?" She winked, like she was trying to be a pretty television star, except it was just a muscle spasm.

Everybody turned away from her.

But the interruption had given my grandmother her escape hatch. She changed the subject and I still didn't understand how Jesus could be God *and* the son of God at the same time.

Santa Claus, she explained, did not *live* in the sky; he flew *through* it once a year on a sleigh powered by reindeer. He lived at the North Pole with Mrs. Claus and some little people who made toys for him.

"You mean midget slaves?" I asked.

My grandmother sucked in her air. "Goodness gracious, no, I most certainly do not mean *midget slaves.*

Where did you even learn to combine such words? These are little leprechauns he has up there with him and—"

My grandfather blasted in. "Aw now, hell, Carolyn, don't go twisting the boy back up in knots all over again now that you finally got him straightened out. They aren't *leprechauns*, son. They're elves. Leprechauns are those little drunk motherfuckers from Ireland."

Carolyn let out a little yelp. "J. G. Robison, I should wash your mouth out with soap, you know better than to use such language in front of a child."

I told my grandmother, "It's okay. We say much worse things here."

Her face grew dark. "You do?"

Jack chuckled into his drink and my grandmother moved on.

Once a year, Santa delivered presents to all the good boys and girls all over the world.

My grandparents had brought a life-size stuffed Santa, not a life-size Jesus. As my grandmother said, "Nobody knows for sure how tall Jesus was, anyway, so he could hardly be life-size, even if he *was* Jesus—which he is not, son. Which he most certainly is not."

I was more confused than ever. "So, Christmas is Jesus's own birthday?"

My grandmother said that it was.

I told her how in stores, sometimes you saw pictures of Jesus, but mostly, you saw Santa. On television, you saw cartoons and programs with both of them. And that's why I figured, *Jesus brings presents to all the poor, foreign, and crippled children and Santa brings presents to the regular children, like me.*

That's what I thought in the beginning, anyway.

"But then I heard this song called, 'Here Comes Santa Claus' and it goes, 'Hang your stockings and *say your prayers,* 'cause Santa Claus comes tonight,' and I realized, 'say your prayers' means they are the same person. It's just that, most of the year, Jesus is naked except for his little rag and his thorn hat and then on Christmas, he puts on his good red suit."

My grandmother stared at me in disbelief. And then she glanced up at my mother as if to say, *This is all your doing.* You could just about see those words right there in her eyes. But my mother didn't catch the look because she was struggling to open a can of tuna at the counter; the opener kept sliding off the lid and banging against the Formica countertop. Frustrated, she finally tossed aside the opener and began stabbing at the lid with a fork until Jack gently placed his hand onto her wrist and smiled at her.

I knew my grandmother thought I was as dumb as a sock, but somehow, this had made perfect sense to me.

It wasn't like I actually sat down and figured the whole thing out. But my beliefs had evolved over time—one piece of false information layered on top of another—until I came to my incorrect and extremely sinful view of Christmas.

Darkly, I thought of all the wordy, bossy letters I had mailed to Jesus—long lists of products that I wanted and where they could be purchased. I'd even lied to him once and said, "My brother says he doesn't want anything and I can have whatever ration you were going to give him, so could I have an above-ground pool?" You weren't supposed to lie, and I had lied to the very man who made up the rule about not lying. I could not even think about how furious these letters must have made him. He's busy building goats and rocks and air and I am pestering him and lying. Jesus, I realized, must just *hate* me.

Sitting on my grandmother's lap as she explained that Jesus and Santa were two entirely different people with very different careers, I felt something drain out of me. *Joy* was bleeding away, being replaced with a kind of cottony confusion and a disappointment that seemed to have a physical weight, like stones.

What else did I believe that was wrong?

Once my grandmother was convinced that I was clear on exactly who was standing beside the tree, she allowed me to jump off her lap and run out to see him. I heard her say to my parents, "What a funny, funny child," as I left the room.

It was two days before Christmas. My parents and grand-parents sat in the kitchen around the table drinking Singapore slings and snacking on appetizers my mother had extracted from cans. My big brother was safely stored away in his bedroom doing the unimaginable.

I found myself alone in the living room with the twinkling Christmas tree and Santa—formerly Jesus—standing right beside it.

I dragged one of the chairs from the dining table over to the tree and climbed up on the seat. Standing, I was now eye-to-eye with Santa.

The sparkling blue eyes were so clear and bright that I was entranced. They looked like real eyes, taken out of a real person and put inside the doll. It was amazing, mesmerizing.

And the beard. And the lips. And just his whole face. It was all so real.

Standing now with my own face just inches from the stuffed Santa, I was trembling with emotion. Did it even *matter* whether he was Jesus or Santa, when one thing was certain: he was all mine?

I leaned forward and kissed him on the cheek. His wax skin felt warm and soft. Not hard and cold, like plastic. But silky, like a candle.

I took a sniff.

He even *smelled* like a candle.

I leaned forward again and this time, I kissed Santa on the lips.

A startling, nearly electric sensation shot through me and I quickly looked over my shoulder to make sure nobody was watching. I knew that Jesus was watching— Carolyn said he saw everything—but I also knew it didn't matter what Jesus thought since I was already going to burn in hell for all of time.

Somehow, I understood that what I was doing was incredibly thrilling and must, therefore, be incredibly wrong.

But I was safe. The grown-ups were still in the kitchen, I could hear them laughing, my grandmother's high-pitched, delighted squeal, "*Oh*, you don't *mean* it!"

I kissed Santa again, and this time I stuck my tongue out and swiped it across Santa's lips.

I didn't know why I did this and the action surprised me. Kissing was something you did with your lips, not your tongue. So what made me do *that*?

I did it again. Sliding my mouth all over Santa's, I licked his upper lip, his lower lip, the corners of his mouth. I licked and licked and licked because not only did Santa smell like a delicious candle, he *tasted* like one, too.

My heart was pounding and I was overwhelmed with new and astonishing sensations and desires. At any moment, my grandmother or my father could poke their head out from the kitchen doorway and see me and I'd be in trouble.

Just one more kiss, I thought, and I leaned forward once again.

With Santa's lips in my mouth, I bit down. I bit down *hard*. His lips came off right in my mouth.

Shocked and unsure of what to *do* now that I had Santa's lips entirely in my mouth, instinct took over and I started to chew.

I chewed the lips and they dissolved almost to nothing. They were, I realized happily, exactly like one of my favorite candies—wax soda bottles, filled with liquid.

I moved to the right where his plump, red check presented an impossibly tempting round knob. I bit it clean off his face, leaving a gaping hole with what appeared to be Styrofoam beneath.

I chewed and swallowed.

I bit off his chin and then I went for his ear, but it

was hard plastic and resisted my teeth, so I settled for a little bit of neck.

His beautiful, true eyes: I opened wide, curled back my lips and bit into the ridge of his brow.

I bit off his nose.

"Why, Margaret, you can't *possibly* mean that!" my grandmother shrieked from the other room, before bursting into peals of laughter. "Oh, but that's just the most precious thing I have ever heard in all my life."

And it was this, the sound of my grandmother's laughter, that lifted me out of my love mist, my strange new hunger, that made me pull away from Santa and look at him again with fresh, clean eyes. And I saw that what I had done had gone alarmingly beyond kissing.

Carefully, silently, I stepped down from the chair and I carried it back to the dining room table.

Even from across the room I could see the carnage that was Santa's face. I'd disfigured him, hideously. I felt sure that even Jesus, with his love for the maimed, would turn away. Santa now looked like his sleigh had crashed on a roof, his face slamming hard into the brick edge of a fireplace chimney.

I'd devastated the life-size Santa.

I began to tremble, this time not with anticipation, unnamed and unknowable excitement, but from dread. I was going to get in a lot of trouble for *this*.

But then, could I maybe hide what I had done?

And I had an idea.

Quietly, I padded back to Santa and I placed my arms on his legs. I turned him counterclockwise so that now, instead of standing beside the tree and looking out into the room, waving at everyone who passed, he was facing the tree and his raised arm made him appear as though he was going to smack the tree, knock it over. Or, I realized dreadfully, he looked like he was about to mess with my mother's special decorations— her nut mouse, her corncob friends.

Still, it was *better.* And when one of them came into the room and made a move to turn him around, I could act like a baby and fuss, *"But I like him better this way. He looks more real. Don't turn him around. Leave him alone! Don't look!"*

Unfortunately, things never progressed that far.

Just a moment later, my mother and Carolyn strolled out of the kitchen and into the living room. I held my breath and prepared for them, the same way you would prepare for a cold wave that's about to hit you at the beach.

"What on earth?" my grandmother gasped.

My mother was staring at my chest. "Augusten, *what* is that mess all over your shirt?"

I looked down and saw bits of fleshy wax, chewed

white hairs, tiny shreds of lip all down the front of my shirt.

My mother lowered herself onto her knees and began to inspect my shirt, brushing the curious crumbs into her open hand and examining them.

My grandmother, I knew without being able to see, was standing before Santa. Her complete silence told me she had seen Santa's face.

My face was hot and I knew it was bright red. Why wouldn't Carolyn say anything? The mangled face had shocked her mute. It had been more awful than I imagined. I might have to go right to hell tonight.

And then finally, she did speak. "Margaret, put Augusten into the Cadillac. We're going to have to drive to the hospital and get his stomach pumped."

I absolutely detested having my arms and legs strapped to the table, but the nurse told me, "It's the only way."

The medical staff gathered around the gurney inserted a terrible, seemingly endless tube down my throat. My mother stood at the back of the room chewing on her fingernails. "But why? *Why*, Augusten?"

It wasn't like I could answer her. At least not until

they removed the thick plastic tube they had snaked into my mouth, down my throat, and into my stomach.

Horribly, I could see the waxy chewed contents of my stomach rising up through the tube and into some sort of pail. Bits of pink lip and fragments of Santa's blue eyes, along with clumps of white beard were sucked out of me, as though modern medicine itself was trying desperately to reverse what I had done and save Christmas.

I was terrified, humiliated, in extreme physical discomfort, and confused. On top of this, the only way I could make the room vanish was to close my eyes. But every time I did, I saw the ghoulish, ruined face of Santa, staring back at me with his questioning, kind eyes. *"Why did you do this to me? I got you the ID bracelet last year, the two-tone just like you wanted,"* he seemed to be saying to me, though of course he no longer had a mouth.

I knew for a fact that I would never receive another Christmas present. And there wasn't a child in the world that would want to sit on Santa's lap now and stare up at his horribly maimed face. He would have to wear a leather face mask now and he would need a seeing-eye dog.

In the recovery room, I thought about all the items on my wish list: the Texas Instruments calculator, the saltwater aquarium with real sharks, the platform shoes. None of it would be mine.

For the rest of my life, I would be on Santa's naughty list, right there at the very top. Mine was the one house he could mark off his list with black, permanent marker.

And Jesus, God's only child, certainly he, too, was watching me from the sky, his eyes narrow with bewilderment, disgust.

I had displeased them both and would be punished.

I'd ruined not only Christmas, but any chance I ever had of getting into heaven. And this realization caused my nose to itch madly but I could not scratch it. Because my hands were still bound to the rails along either side of the hospital bed. I may have been lying flat on clean white sheets, but I was most certainly crucified.

And Two Eyes Made
Out of Coal

OR AS LONG as I could remember my mother would buy an intricate, often handcrafted advent calendar and hang it on the refrigerator. It was she who introduced me to the concept of a calendar for the month of December, a countdown to Christmas. Where each date from *1* to *25* was printed on a little door you could open. And behind the door, a visual surprise—a little scene or charming sketch. I wanted nothing more than to sit on the floor with the thing and tear off all the doors at once so I could get immediately to Christmas.

I had, over the years, developed something more than a fondness for the paper calendar. Each Christmas when the calendar went up, I stopped *living* and started *waiting*. My mother surely must have regretted ever introducing me to the advent calendar, because now she could never take it away. It would be like getting your child hooked on heroin and then withholding their needle.

Only one row of doors remained closed on the advent calendar. For the last eighteen days, it had been the single focus of my life. My mother would not allow me to open a new door before eight o'clock in the evening. By seven each night, I was sitting on the floor in front of the refrigerator like a dog, staring up at the calendar and asking her every few minutes, "Is it almost eight o'clock?"

Always, there was a fleeting disappointment upon opening the door because the image revealed was never one I recognized. "What is that? What does some old man on a camel have to do with Christmas?"

My mother leaned over to inspect the image in question and then she explained. "Oh, look at that! What a beautiful image. See, now I believe these are actually woodblock prints behind the doors. But done with such fine, fine detail. I would love to be able to achieve a line like that," she said, pointing to the hump on the camel's back.

"But what *is* it?"

"Well, this is one of the Three Wise Men, I imagine.

On his way to see Jesus. Or maybe he's just riding around in the desert for some fresh air. Look at the way they captured the wind on the sand, it's gorgeous. You know, I bought this calendar from Faces in Amherst. It's German. I wish I'd picked up those napkin rings while I was there."

By this point, I was no longer listening to her and was instead focused on the next night's door. Surely, there was something better under *that* door.

The last week was always the worst. It was like an unbearable itch I could not reach. "You have waited patiently for three hundred and forty-five days and you only have one more week," my mother would tell me.

But somehow, this one week seemed longer than all the others combined. So I was constantly seeking a distraction, but one that was related to Christmas. My mother helped by offering to sit with me and string cranberries and popcorn together into long garlands for the tree. We each had a needle and thread as we sat before the television set with a large bowl of popcorn and a bag of fresh cranberries on the table between us.

But even this couldn't go on for a week. "Oh my God, you need to put that mess down now and go wash your hands and put some Band-Aids on your fingers."

"But I don't want to stop. I can keep going. We need more."

"Augusten, you are going to get blood all over the house. You have just pricked your fingers to death with that sewing needle. And see? Look at that; your entire rope of popcorn is bloody. You don't want to hang bloody popcorn on the tree, do you?"

"Mine can go in the back!" I said, protectively clutching the needle and thread and bloody popcorn rope to my chest.

She shook her head, no. "Go wash your hands. And use some Bactine before you put on the Band-Aids."

The stores had begun filling their shelves with Christmas decorations way back in October, so along with jack-o'-lanterns and paper turkeys, you could buy a can of spray snow.

By this point, I had burned through numerous cans, even though my father paid good money to have the real stuff removed from our driveway and front steps.

I had sprayed it on my bedroom windows, adding a string of wildly blinking lights. Tinsel, my favorite product, was draped from anything in my room that protruded even slightly: the needle arm of my record player, curtain rods, the switch to my desk lamp. My room was a festering, glittering shrine in honor of my favorite day of the year. But there were only so many times I could move my own small artificial Christmas tree from one side of the room to the other. At a certain point during that last painful week, I simply ran out of preholiday amusements.

So I would wander into the living room to at least be in the same room with the real tree. As it had for weeks, my scratchy copy of *A Charlie Brown Christmas* continued to moan away on the record player.

Because all the magazines that had arrived featured Christmas trees and stockings and other holiday paraphernalia on their covers, I would thumb through these, searching only for the colorful ads.

This was what I was doing the Saturday morning before Christmas, while my parents were downstairs sleeping. On Saturdays, it was rare for them to come upstairs before ten or even noon. That gave me a good five to seven hours alone.

Upstairs.

With complete, unsupervised access to a fully equipped kitchen.

The photograph on the cover of my mother's *Woman's Day* magazine appealed to me enormously. A gumdrop-bejeweled gingerbread house from a spun-sugar fantasy world.

The tall, peaked roof was swirled with mounds of frosting snow. Glittering, crystal-sugar icicles hung from the eaves. And the walls, smooth sheets of pure gingerbread had been pressed into raw sugar, giving them the appearance of stucco.

Hansel and Gretel had been fools to abandon such a house after they cooked the witch alive in her own oven. I absolutely would have claimed the house as my own and used the witch's skull as a soup tureen. When I thought about it, Hansel and Gretel deserved to die for their lack of imagination and poor real estate choices. But that was just a stupid fantasy; a story for babies.

This gingerbread house was real. There was a recipe. GINGERBREAD DREAMS: BUILD THIS FOOLPROOF FANTASY HOUSE! directed the headline.

I would make it as a surprise for my mother. I would bake the gingerbread house and I wouldn't get any blood on it and it would be the center of our Christmas table. *Won't she be surprised*, I thought, *when she comes upstairs in six hours and sees my glorious gingerbread house resting on a plate, two candy cane trees beside the front door!*

The word *foolproof* spoke to me because my older brother often said, "I believe you may be a complete fool, quite nearly retarded. I'm going to have to find out what kind of pesticides were in use when our mother was carrying you." If even a fool could make the house on the cover of this magazine, I should be able to make it, too. Then again, I knew that merely boiling water was not *foolproof.* Not when you got sidetracked by *Fat Albert and the Cosby Kids* and forgot about the water, which then evaporated and the pot fused to the burner of the stove.

Had they actually tested this recipe on a fool? I wondered.

But this was no pot of boiling water. This was only gingerbread! And gumdrops! It was just plain silly to be *worried* about candy canes. No, the gingerbread house would look exactly like the one on the magazine cover. I knew it would.

I loved to experiment in the kitchen and if I ever used a recipe, it was only for inspiration. Recipes, I felt, were for the unimaginative. However, with this particular project I would do my best to follow the recipe to the letter. And where that wasn't possible, I would at least stay true to its spirit.

Molasses, whatever the hell that was, sure wasn't in our cupboard. But I knew it was a liquid because you were supposed to "gently pour" it into the other ingredients, so I used some of my mother's cooking sherry—something she herself often incorporated into fancier recipes.

We had flour. Because the gingerbread house was gingerbread colored, I used the brown flour made out of wheat and not the other flour made out of white.

And wasn't baking *soda* the same thing as baking *powder*? I thought so, so I used the latter.

As for the spices—cinnamon, cardamom, nutmeg, ginger, fennel—I skipped them all. Because right there next to the Tabasco sauce and peeking out from behind a bottle of my mother's saccharin was a little jar of allspice. Just the name tasted like gingerbread. It was all the spices I needed plus the rest of them. It was all of them; allspice!

Briefly, I worried about the spectacular mess I had somehow created. I had managed to use my mother's entire set of six white mixing bowls, her electric beater, a number of pans, each of which I had greased with corn oil, and assorted spatulas, knives, forks, a cheese grater, and my father's hammer from the basement.

It was just a shame that I wouldn't be able to help my mother wash all these dishes, but I couldn't get all my Band-Aids wet so she would have to do them herself.

I smiled.

She always said that art was born from chaos. "The creative process can be very messy. You have to be comfortable with that."

I was comfortable.

I poured the thick, gluey batter onto trays and baked it stiff. Prying the gingerbread, which was nearly black, from the cookie sheets, I set about to assemble my Gingerbread Dreams Fantasy House.

Gloomily, I came to accept the fact that it was a structural impossibility to create a steep, peaked roof, like in the picture. The gingerbread kept breaking. The instant coffee I had added for color must have made it brittle.

So I gave the building a flat roof—like the modern house down the street that my mother often admired— and then spent an hour applying white frosting from a can for snow. Which looked nothing like mounds of snow, but like piles of insulation left behind by a work crew that had gone on strike. It looked, actually, just like the house even *farther* down the street; the one built in the center of a dirt field. With plastic stapled to the outside in place of siding and asphalt nailed here and there to patch holes. My mother hated that house. "It ruins the entire damn street."

I had made *that* house, in black gingerbread. If only I had two miniature flat tires and an upside-down swing set to place in front.

I cut out more windows. Two rows of them. Immediately, this looked wrong. It looked *nonresidential.*

The deeper into the project I tumbled, the more dire the results. The colorful gumdrops I'd attached randomly to the front façade didn't look *cheerful,* they looked like what they were: an easy, colorful ploy to manipulate the eye and distract it from the wanton ugliness right before it. The more I did to try and decorate my way out of the monstrosity I had built, the worse it looked.

By not even the most elastic stretch of the imagination was this a gingerbread *house.*

Four walls, a flat ceiling, rows of windows, four stories high: I had built a gingerbread public housing tenement, a little gingerbread slum.

And I could populate my small-scale confectionary representation of urban blight with the deformed gingerbread men that I had baked alongside the cake. Men with misshapen arms and legs, heads that had expanded into great amoebalike structures. I had baked an entire population of pitiful, armless and legless subjects, each

44

with a physical deformity worthy of the most corrupt circus.

I didn't even bother to frost my gingerbread misfits. Why shame them with frivolous frosting hats and raisin eyes? Let them be plain and blind. I could give them *that* much dignity.

I would think of them as a large family who had, unfortunately, farmed too near a leaking nuclear power plant. And now they only wanted to live the remainder of their sad lives in the solitude of the cookie jar and not displayed on a platter near my public housing unit.

It was almost like I had baked a scene from the *CBS Evening News* with Walter Cronkite.

My mother made a bold and insincere fuss. "Oh, it's just precious," she said. *Precious* being the word southern women have always used to describe the indescribable, the unsavory. It's also what my grandmother had said after peering at the harelip on the baby of a friend's daughter. *Precious* meant *So positively hideous, I could produce vomit this instant and without the aid of my index finger.*

45

She was reduced to bland compliments. "It's so *original*. I like it very much more than the picture in the magazine."

When I asked her, "But doesn't it look like one of the slums on the news? Like something out of Springfield?" she replied, "No, honey, not at all." But I could see in her eyes the distinct flicker of recognition and then agreement. Her eyes said, *Exactly!*

I knew that what I had constructed was an insult to the picture in the magazine, to the entire magazine itself and to baking in general. If the people at *Woman's Day* ever saw my gingerbread horror they would cancel my mother's subscription.

Why hadn't I followed the directions *exactly*? Why had I thrown the measuring cups to the wind and decided to spread my architectural wings?

Worse, though, than the visual presentation was the sensation of the gingerbread house inside the mouth.

First, the teeth made hard, damaging contact with the bathroom tilelike cake. Next, the tongue was burned by the cheap, hardened vanilla frosting. A single bite was enough to onset juvenile diabetes.

Still, the front door and a tiny portion of roof were politely sampled. A number of gumdrops had been removed, then placed back. The dog refused a chunk of window even though it was caked with frosting "snow."

This very same dog did not hesitate to eat the wadded-up ball of aluminum foil she found on the floor next to the trash can.

And so my fiasco sat in ruin on a platter in the center of the dining table. Now no longer a food item but a stand-in for a decoration.

And then my brother appeared. He had briefly left his bedroom and all the electronic equipment in there to forage for food.

With one swift and decisive motion of the hand, he cracked a third of the roof away from the structure and got as much of it into his mouth as possible before I could scream at him and tell him to stop. But I wasn't going to scream at him. My mouth was open in amazement, not anger. I was just waiting for him to snarl in disgust and spit the partially chewed roof right out onto the floor.

"You like it?" I asked, amazed.

He shrugged. "It's okay, I guess. Why, did you put something funny in it?" he said suspiciously, holding the last corner of roof out away from him.

"No, it's edible," I said. "There's no tricks."

He nodded. Then he devoured the fragment in his hand and returned to the cake for more, breaking away nearly one entire wall of my holiday housing unit.

"Well, since nobody else is gonna eat it," he said,

carrying the wall away with him down the hall and back to his room.

I looked at the wretched structure on the table and I smiled. My gingerbread hovel had suddenly turned in to a loved—or at least somewhat appreciated—gingerbread *home* after all.

Claus and Effect

*A*T MY ELEMENTARY school, the teachers always did a little something special to celebrate everyone's birthday. About an hour before the yellow buses arrived to take us home at the end of the day, one of the teachers would unroll the torn but taped-back-together crinkly red paper streamer that was used over and over, year after year, and hang it from one end of the chalkboard to the other. HAPPY BIRTHDAY would be written in neat teacher-script on the board. And a couple of boxes of Twinkies would be opened and placed on the long fake wood table below the streamer and chalkboard sign. Apple juice would be poured into tiny paper cups from a half-gallon plastic jug. It was a small school in the country; such a make-shift little party was exciting for everyone.

Except for Glen.

Sooner or later, after the juice cups had been crumpled up and pelted at the girls and the last Twinkie was gone, somebody would always say, "Poor Glen, he never gets a party." And this never failed to plunge the room into silence. "Yeah, that's right. Hey Glen, that really sucks."

The two Brendas and a couple of other girls would walk over to Glen and put their hands on his shoulder, petting him lightly, as one would a bony and pitiful dog. Because of all their work with dolls, young girls could be shockingly maternal; they could confuse you and make you cry and want a grilled cheese sandwich.

Glen, embarrassed by the clutch of empathetic girls and annoyed that the spotlight had once again been aimed at him would laugh uncomfortably and say, "It's no big deal. I don't care, really. I never do anything for my birthday anyway."

And all of us would then hold our breath because Glen had spoken the unspeakable.

Glen had a disability more disfiguring than a burn and more terrifying than cancer.

Glen had been born on the day after Christmas.

"My parents just combine my birthday with Christmas, that's all," he explained.

But we knew this was a lie. Glen's parents just wrapped a couple of his Christmas presents in birthday-themed wrapping paper, stuck some candles in a supermarket cake, and had a dinner of Christmas leftovers.

Mrs. Sobel had tried to make Glen feel less like a hobbled cripple by telling him, "I know just how it is, honey. My mother was born on Pearl Harbor day."

Everybody had just stared at her vacantly until Andi ruined it for everybody by raising her hand and saying, "My mother has pearls. She got them from her mother and she says when I'm grown-up, I'll get to have them."

That was how Mrs. Sobel discovered that none of us had ever heard the words *pearl* and *harbor* combined before. Thus began a two-week social studies project where we learned about the fateful day and were each forced to paint our own small corner of a wall mural depicting bombs falling from the sky and sinking boats at one end and Japanese kids throwing Frisbees at the other, but none of us had ever seen a Japanese kid before, so they were drawn like what we saw in cartoons: black, jagged hair, two slanted slashes for eyes, and a karate robe. Mrs. Sobel approved and suggested a Japanese flag be added to the headband.

In the corner, hidden by an explosion, I had slyly drawn an oyster with a pearl inside. I had written, "Don't kill me, I'm so pretty!" as a tiny thought bubble coming from the pearl.

Everybody had silently blamed Glen for this art project, a task we considered punishment. Still, nobody could really *hate* him for it the way they could hate, say, Allison Murray because she was always telling on everyone. Life itself had punished Glen enough already.

I knew that I would rather spend the rest of my life in a wheelchair like one of Jerry's Kids than suffer through life with a birthday the day after Christmas.

Sure, other kids had lousy birthdays, too. Like Mark, whose birthday was in the no-man's-land of *March,* or that hog-faced Bertha from up in the fourth grade who was born on February second—Groundhog Day. But these were just run-of-the-mill cruddy birthdays.

Glen suffered an actual birth defect. And that's why no matter whose birthday we were celebrating, it was always Glen who went home with the last Twinkie, even though he protested. "Aw, c'mon, don't make me take it, please? It's bad enough already with everybody feeling so sorry for me."

"Nonsense," the teacher would say, cramming the greasy, cream-filled sponge log into his backpack while we all looked at him with pity, weak smiles on our lips, tears glittering in the teacher's eyes.

But because there is the slum in India, so, too, must there be Beverly Hills.

I had an October birthday. October twenty-third. This was the calendar's finest piece of real estate. Mine was the Rodeo Drive of birthdays.

The *only-in-the-way* spring birthdays were long past as were those pesky, mosquito-bitten summer birthdays. September was a somber month as summer's death was mourned. But by mid-October everyone was suddenly ready for the fall.

The air was refreshing. People were excited about Halloween. But they were not distracted by it, consumed with it. They were not cutting down trees and making lists and worrying about money. Everybody was happy because everybody—even the grown-ups—would soon get to have some candy.

And when you had a birthday on October twenty-third, there was always something to talk about at your birthday party: "What are you gonna be this year? I was a bat last year. I'm going as a toothbrush this time." Plus, nobody could skimp on your presents because you were still far enough away from Christmas.

I didn't care a thing about Halloween. In fact, it always made me feel a little foolish. It seemed to me that if you were going to be in costume, there should be a studio audience. I saw my October birthday merely as the very first step on the grand staircase to Christmas.

But I lived for Christmas.

And once my birthday arrived, it was only one slippery week until Halloween had come and gone. And then there was nothing in the way of Christmas.

If you didn't count that annoying Thanksgiving, which I absolutely did not.

I despised those pilgrims with their buckle shoes and their coffin clothes. I resented having to study them in class and then be forced to delay Christmas festivities until their stupid canned-cranberry-sauce holiday was over.

Likewise, I hated the Indians for not slaughtering them all.

Thanksgiving was nothing more than a pilgrim-created obstacle in the way of Christmas; a dead bird in the street that forced a brief detour.

While I no longer believed in Santa at the age of nine, I did believe in *giving*.

And as far as I was concerned, my parents would give me whatever I wanted. It was my payment for enduring the other 364 days of the year with them. Between my nasty drunk father and my suicidal, mental-patient mother, I felt I was owed certain reimbursements. They had aged me; I would drain them dry.

Beginning December first, I became like a young network executive; trying to organize a thousand different things at once, establishing lists of priorities, creating fallback plans and passing these documents along to those who *would make it happen*—my parents.

"It's just a first draft," I told them as they sat stone-faced at the kitchen table, my mother's strained, medicated eyes focused on the salt and pepper shakers and my father, as usual, barely glancing up from his college students' exam booklets.

I slid the document onto the table between them. Neatly printed along the top was the title, STOCKING STUFFERS: YOUR OPTIONS, followed by a list of acceptable items.

14K gold electroplate LED watch (Mountain Farms Mall)
OR
Bag of coins (quarters and above)
OR
Real gold nuggets (5–6)
AND
Real leather wallet (filled with assortment of bills)
Variety of candy (chocolate, *NO fruit-based candies*)
Red candy canes, not green NO MINT OR
WINTERGREEN ANYTHING
AND
Level B surprise gift—Mother-selected
Assortment of level C gifts—Mother-selected

A second sheet of paper was provided featuring a list of lower-priced B items, such as sterling-silver neck chains, mood rings, Silly Putty, and finally a C list of gums, Jawbreakers, and other under-a-dollar items, most of which could cause cavities or stain fabric. I had to specify *mother-selected* because if my father chose the gifts, they would be grossly inappropriate for the era.

Last year, my stocking was filled with brittle cellophane-wrapped packages of Lance Toastchee peanut butter and cheese crackers. Then into the toe of the stocking my father had crammed a useless nickel with a lumpy cow on the back.

Worst of all, he'd included three unsharpened pencils.

"*Well,* these are the presents I used to receive in my stocking when I was your age," he said. And he didn't look mad about it, either. He looked all happy and dippy, like he always did when he remembered his own kid things.

"Jack and Carolyn gave you a bunch of junky crackers and that's it?" I asked, astonished.

"*Junky?* These were brand new back then. Why, nobody had ever seen anything like them! Crackers with real cheese and peanut butter inside? It was amazing. Like a sandwich you could carry around in your pocket. I took a package with me to my classroom and showed the other kids and boy oh boy, were they envious."

I looked at the fifteen or twenty packs of crackers I'd dumped out on the carpet. Our dog, Cream, had come over and sniffed them and she had walked away. "Well, then you can have these, too," I said, sliding the mound of them toward his rocking chair. And without comment, I slid the pencils toward him, too.

"You don't want your pencils?" he said, stunned, like I was handing him back a crisp fifty. "Those are *number-one* lead pencils. We used to fight over those in school."

"Yeah, so do the kids at my school. Only they fight *with* them. Eric got stabbed in the eardrum. That's why we have to use those Flair felt tips now."

He considered this.

"And the nickel? That was your big present?" I asked sourly, pinching the dirty coin between my thumb and index finger like I would a dead roach.

"Son, that's not just a nickel. It's an Indian Head nickel. You don't see too many of these anymore. Did you turn it over?" he asked, reaching from his chair.

I turned it over and shrugged. Then I crawled across the carpet, too lazy to stand, and handed it to him.

He chuckled as he inspected the coin. "Yes, yes,

there it is. See? The buffalo on the other side. A great big old buffalo, how about that?"

"I thought it was just a cow," I said, bored. "I get those animal nickels in change sometimes. I always throw them in the trash because I thought they were counterfeit."

My father nearly swallowed his tongue. "You th-th-threw away your Indian Head nickels?"

"Well, yeah. How was I supposed to know they were real? The only animal allowed on regular American money is that bird. We don't put farm animals on the money anymore."

My father said, "Well, I cannot imagine. When I was your age, we used to beg my mother for her change purse so we could hunt for Indian Heads. If I had been given one in change? Why, that would have been the happiest day of my life."

He looked truly bewildered, lost in time. It was like I had informed him, "Yes, and not only do the horses now have *engines* strapped to their stomachs? But their legs have been chopped off and replaced with wheels!"

So this year, I wanted to make sure I didn't wake up on Christmas morning and find another stocking filled with more junk from his childhood—nails, paper clips, rocks. It amazed me that he loved Christmas almost as much as me, though for clearly different reasons.

My father studied my documents. "Gold nuggets!" he

said, alarmed. "What on earth are you going to do with gold nuggets?"

I said, "Polish them. *Have* them. I don't know. I just want them, that's all."

Now he removed his reading glasses. "Well, son, I don't think you would be as happy with gold nuggets as you think. Often, this natural gold that you want, these nuggets, as you call them, are contaminated with pieces of rock—almost a kind of dirt—and—"

"What do you mean, *dirt?*" I said. "Gold doesn't come with dirt stuck on it. I've seen pictures."

He said, "No, that's not true, now. Gold does indeed sometimes have little pebbles mixed in with it. And even a kind of dirt. It's not especially pretty. They have to melt it down to make rings and whatnot."

I looked at him with my eyes narrowed to see if I could detect a lie. He sounded suspiciously like my older brother, who lied constantly about everything. It had been my brother who told me there was no such thing as Santa Claus. "Not anymore there's not," he'd said. "Santa worked in the off-season at a shipyard in Amsterdam and he was killed in a forklift accident."

I'd been mortified and believed him unquestionably. Only that night because I asked my father where they'd buried Santa's body did I learn the truth. He wasn't really dead. He never existed.

Having already believed for many years that Santa and Jesus were the same person, I was kind of relieved to actually be done with him. He never really had made any sense to me.

But my father did not appear to be playing a trick on me.

"Can't you wash it off?" I asked.

"I'm afraid not, son," he said. "The little pieces of rock are embedded within the gold."

I snatched my list back and crossed out *Gold nuggets.* "Okay, forget those," I said. Then I wrote in *Gold bars.*

All my father said was, "I don't know about that."

I raised my eyebrows in challenge. As far as I was concerned, Christmas was my yearly paycheck and I wasn't about to accept any deductions.

"Did I ever tell you," he said now, leaning back in his chair, "about the year I received a chimp as a Christmas present?"

Now I was certain he was lying and I didn't find it funny. "You never had a chimp."

"I most surely did. Your grandfather bought it for me overseas and he had it shipped all the way to Lawrenceville, Georgia. We kept it in a big ol' cage in the backyard. Boy, was that one mean chimp. If you tried to get up close to him, he'd be liable to pee on you. And if you went anywhere near the bars, he'd try and bite you. Oh, he was just a mean, nasty animal."

"You kept it in a cage?" And I imagined a little person-monkey dressed in overalls and tap shoes, clutching a harmonica in one hand and a banana in the other, being jammed into a cage.

"We had to. Son, this was a wild, wild animal, taken from its home in nature. Not some TV chimp dressed up in human clothing and trained to do silly tricks," he said, with disdain.

I said, "You never mind the outfits and the tricks, can you still get chimps as pets?"

He told me he wasn't sure, but he expected that you could. Although you would be foolish to want one. "People are under the false impression, from these TV animals, that chimps are fun, almost human companions. Well, I can personally tell you that they are aggressive, hateful creatures that throw their own bowel movements at you. They growl and snap like the worst dog imaginable. They are just terrible, terrible animals."

Of course, I knew this was untrue. I knew the monkey only resented the cage and the pencil-twirling Goody Two-shoes that came out once in a while to inspect it. A chimp needed love and tenderness, just like a person. It also needed a glitter headband, a bib, and a tambourine.

I once again snatched my paper back and scribbled *Monkey?* in the corner. "I have to revise this," I told him. "I'll have a fresh copy for you in the morning."

"Margaret!" my father shouted. "Stop your damn daydreaming."

My mother startled and looked up from the salt and pepper shakers, seeing me for the first time. "Hey there," she said, smiling warmly. "Do you have a fever?"

"No, Margaret, he doesn't have a damn *fever.* He's been standing here for well over five minutes with his little Christmas list. How you could not see that is beyond my understanding."

My mother reached for her pack of cigarettes and pulled one out. She placed it into her mouth and then turned toward my father and extended her face. She closed her eyes like she was expecting a kiss.

My father lit her cigarette.

"Listen, you bastard," she began, blowing the smoke right in his face. "I do not need to be attacked by you today. I am on a new medication and it makes me feel very cotton-blooded."

"It's cotton-headed, you madwoman, the expression is cotton-*headed.* Now, I was just telling little Augusten here about my pet chimp. I'm not sure he believes I even had one."

My mother turned and looked at me. "Oh, your father had a chimpanzee all right. It *hated* him. Now, it may not be as exotic as a captive primate, but one year my daddy gave me a goat for Christmas."

"Oh, not this damn story again," my father said.

My mother didn't even look at him. She just kind of talked over her shoulder at him, her eyes on the ceiling. "John. Gordon. Robison. The day I can have those words carved onto a headstone will be the happiest of my life." Then she looked back at me. "It was a scruffy, scrappy little billy goat and I absolutely adored it!"

"Wait, you got a goat for Christmas? But you didn't live on a farm."

"Of course I didn't live on a *farm*," my mother said, bringing her hand protectively to her neck. She laughed at the absurdity of the notion, as though I had asked her if her first boyfriend had been a rooster. "Daddy owned pecan orchards. Oh, just acres and acres of the most beautiful orchards you ever saw in your life. That's why your grandmother, Amah, sends a box of pecans up here each year for Christmas and I make pie."

My mother's pecan pie. My mouth began to water and I needed to spit. "You aren't going to make that pie again, are you?" I asked, trying to make it sound casual.

My mother was not fooled. "*Once.* I used salt instead of sugar just once."

My father said, "N-now, I think it was more than once.

63

I think maybe it was once or twice. Because I distinctly remember the year your friend from Portland flew out here, the unattractive girl with the facial hair. The artist?"

My mother glared at him. "Are you referring to Nadia?"

My father broke out into a smile and then he laughed. "Why yes! That's exactly the one. Nadia. What an unfortunate appearance that young woman has."

"You are aware that Nadia ended up marrying Clark Hayes, the head of the mathematics department out there at the University of California, aren't you?" my mother asked. "We met Clark, John. Don't you remember? Nice young man. About ten years younger than you? Surely, you remember. You both talked about your freshman students."

She rose from the table and went to the sink, turning the faucet on. She stuck her cigarette under the stream of water to extinguish it and then she dropped the wet butt into the trash can. "Yes, nice Mr. Hayes. Half your age and head of the department."

She stretched, placing her hands on her lower back. "Well, I need a nap. My body has not adjusted to these pills."

"Wait," I shouted.

Inspiration had struck.

In my fussiest little boy voice I complained, "This

isn't *fair.* You got a goat and you got a monkey. And last year you gave me a bunch of stupid *crackers?*"

My mother couldn't help herself, she smiled victoriously and shot my father a look. "I told you, John. When you brought those crackers home I said, 'Do you not know our son?' That's exactly what I said to you."

Finally, I blurted out, "I want a horse. I want my own horse. A real one, not some stupid plastic horse like the girls bring to school. I want a real horse, a new one. Not some old used thing, either. A new horse with a saddle and a leash."

Both of them were silent.

"A pony," I added. "I want a pony."

Then, to emphasize the finality of my decision, I crumpled my list before their eyes and I threw it into the trash. I started to walk out of the room but turned around once more before leaving. "I better get that pony," I said. "Or both of you will regret it."

As I walked down the hall toward my bedroom I heard my mother say, "Well, now you have done it. You and that damn monkey story of yours."

The last thing I heard before closing myself inside my room with my Burl Ives *Have a Holly Jolly Christmas* album was my father: "I was only telling him how terrible a pet that monkey made. I never mentioned anything about a damn horse."

At Caldor, where my mother and I went shopping for gifts for her friends, she kept trying to tempt me away from my pony, which I had now secretly named Al Capone. "Look at this beautiful gold neck chain," she said at the jewelry counter. "Augusten, did you see this? I think it's called a snake chain."

I looked at it from the corner of my eyes. "Yeah, it's a snake chain. With a lobster-claw clasp. I already have one. And mine's electroplated, not *filled* like *that*." My tone was snotty and contemptuous and a normal mother would have spanked such a child or taken him home and drown him in the bathtub.

The child of such people has little choice but to resort to petty manipulations and threats. And in some way, she seemed to know this.

Still, aisle after aisle she tried to unhook my little fists from the reins. "Oh, what a beautiful stereo," she said, running her hands over the plastic lid of the turntable. "And isn't that one of those fancy new eight-track players?"

I ignored her.

"Say, how would you like to have that in your room? Oh, imagine! A gumball machine!"

I said, "Maybe you should make one of your pecan pies this year."

She brightened. "Would you like one? Would you, really? Oh, I would love to make another pecan pie."

"Horses like salt," I said. "They lick it."

She glared at me and pushed the cart forward.

Store after store, day after day, both of my parents tried to interest me in other, more ordinary gifts. My father, pitifully, even dragged me with him to Hastings to get refills for his Parker ballpoint pen. "Son, have a look at this," he said. He was standing before the glass counter in front. I scanned the contents inside but couldn't imagine what it was he wanted me to see.

"Now, I'm sure it's very expensive, but as a special Christmas present, well, you never know. Just maybe Santa would bring you one of those," and he tapped the glass with his finger.

I said, "*That?* On top?"

And my father smiled.

To make absolutely certain I said, "In the white box?"

"That's real gold, son."

I looked at him and I said, "If you get me that for Christmas? You'd also have to get me a Zippo lighter, just like the one you have."

He had begun to smile, but now his smile had turned

into a question mark. "What would you need with a Zippo lighter, son?"

I began to drift away from the counter, trailing my finger down the length of the glass display case. "I would use it to light the house on fire after I opened your Cross pen set *for ladies.*"

My father nearly seemed insulted. "This is no pen set *for ladies!*" he insisted. Then he turned to the clerk. "This set of Cross pens, right here in front. That's not designed for ladies, is it?"

The clerk replied with a nod.

"It *is?* It's for ladies?"

I was standing in front of the cigarettes. "Excuse me," I said to the guy behind the counter. "Could I see a Zippo lighter? Just like my father's." Then I shouted to him: "Hey Dad! Take your Zippo out and show the guy behind the counter so he can see which one."

We were back in the car not even five minutes later. My father was just disgusted. "They should really mark those things clearly. I might easily have purchased that for my damn self and then I would walk around signing documents at the university with this effeminate pen."

The rest of the way home we listened to Christmas music on the radio. "Jingle Bells" and "Deck the Halls" were performed back-to-back with acoustic guitars. My father hated it. "Well, this is just terrible Christmas music, it sounds like that damn Joan Bylezz your mother is always playing. A pipe organ sounds so much nicer."

"Baez," I corrected. "Not *lezz*."

During the station break the announcer said, "Here we are folks, just six more days left until Christmas. And that reminds me of a song. So get comfortable, and get ready. Because Christmas morning will be here before you know it."

On the first day of Christmas my true love gave to me . . .

I sang along, intentionally messing up the words: *"One brand-new pony and a partridge in a pear tree."*

There was a certain tension in the air on Christmas morning. It was not yet seven and I'd been up for two hours. My parents had forced me to wait until seven and now that it was exactly seven, I was in the living room, just beside the fireplace. I looked at the tree. Then I looked at the stockings hanging beside me.

I knew my brother would wake up in five hours, walk over to the fireplace, and lift up his T-shirt, then dump the candy from his stocking onto his shirt, making a sort of hammock. He would then retreat to his bedroom where he would remain until dinner.

I reached into his stocking and felt around. I located a few chocolate gold coins, which I unwrapped and popped into my mouth. I crumpled up the foil and tossed this back into his stocking so that he would see it.

There were lots of presents under the tree.

But not a single one was shaped like a pony.

My parents came into the room, smiling. "Merry Christmas," my mother said. "Yes," my father said, enthusiastically, "a merry, merry Christmas to you, son."

Their grins were so wide, it was clear they were disguises. I said, "Merry Christmas. Is it outside in the backyard?"

Neither of them spoke. "Is what in the backyard?" my mother asked with make-believe innocence.

I scanned their faces. They both lit cigarettes at the same time.

For the next thirty minutes, I sat on the floor beneath the tree opening present after present; more presents than in previous years—too many presents, really.

walkie-talkies, an O-scale Lionel Santa Fe train set, an LED watch, gold electroplated.

Every single thing I had wanted.

I clenched my teeth together to maintain my dour expression.

My mother sat on the sofa and my father was in his rocking chair. They exchanged worried glances at each other across the coffee table. And finally, my mother spoke. "Augusten? I know you had it in your head that you wanted a horse. But we simply do not have the land for a horse. And neither your father nor I know the first thing about them. It's a huge responsibility and they are terribly expensive, more than cars. I did check. I really did. But there's just no way we could get you a horse. Mrs. Clayton down the hill told me you are more than welcome to walk down there after school anytime you want next spring and you can visit her horses."

Now my father interjected. "Son, a horse is just way, way too much animal. If you wanted, say, a goldfish or a turtle? That might be a different story. But even a goldfish would need care and maintenance."

My mother cleared her throat.

And my father said, "Yes, that's right. And the other thing, son, is that when I was given a monkey for Christmas as a little boy, you have to understand, those were very different times. It's not like it is today. People back then didn't have the fiscal responsibilities they have—"

"Oh for heaven's sake, John, he doesn't need a lecture on economics. Why can't you just say what we said you would say? Is that so damn difficult?"

"Now, I have to put up with your constant barrage of criticism every damn day of the year. Am I not allowed one goddamned day of the year where there is some peace and quiet? Or are you going to jump down my back over every damn thing I say?"

"Oh, you are such an infantile man, do you know that? This isn't your goddamned holiday, it's Augusten's. Christmas is for children, not sorry, raging alcoholics. Just because you are miserable at the university doesn't entitle you to terrorize us on Christmas morning."

As they continued to fight, their voices gradually rising until my mother was eventually screaming at full volume, red-faced and furious, I sat on the floor amid a crinkled, reflective sea of wrapping paper and glittering bows. In my hands was a small, hard plastic case, about the size of a book of matches. Inside the case was a little block of white foam. And pressed into this foam were three tiny gold nuggets.

Finally, I could no longer restrain myself. I jumped up and began to dance around the room. I hopped to my brother's stocking and unhooked the candy cane. I bit into it, right through the wrapper, which I spit out onto the floor with expert skill.

"Hey, now!" my father called. "That belongs to your brother."

"He hates candy canes," I shrieked. "Hates, hates, hates, hates them!" And I jumped up onto the fireplace hearth, bit into the candy cane again and then hopped back down. I ran into the center of the wrapping paper and began to kick and dance. Chunks of torn paper and ribbons landed at my parents' feet.

They said nothing. They just looked at me.

At last, my mother said, "Augusten, you are just wild. What has gotten into you? I thought you were depressed about not getting your pony."

I burst into peals of laughter. I threw my head back and clutched the gold to my chest. "Oh my God," I cried. "I never wanted any *dumb, stinky old horse.* Don't you people even know me?" I paused to take two more large bites of the cane. And then I explained, "Horses are for girls and glue factories."

The two of them watched me, wide eyed and nearly terrified.

"Thank you for my presents. You gave me just *exactly* what I wanted. You are officially free to kill each other! Your account has been paid in full for the entire year."

Then I winked at them like one of the hideous, artificial child actors I studied on television and tried, hourly, to replicate in front of the mirror.

My mother's hand had remained utterly motionless, the lit cigarette between her fingers poised in midair just before her lips. Ash from the end dropped down the front of her bathrobe. She was studying me like I was a cat splayed open on her lab tray.

"Well, well," she said finally, clapping very slowly, the cigarette parked between her lips, her eyes squinting against the rising smoke. "Bravo, you hateful spoiled thing."

I beamed at her and curtsied like a girl.

"Now wait one minute here. Are you saying, you changed your mind about the horse?" my father asked. "You didn't want those gold pens instead, did you son? Because I didn't get those pens, I was under the impression you were not interested in them once you found out they were for ladies."

My mother stared at him. "It is a wonder that you are employed by an institution of higher learning. Truly. It is as mysterious as gravity itself."

"Aw, now what the hell are you talking about, nut-woman?"

I sauntered around them, dropping ribbons and scraps of wrapping paper on top of their heads.

"It means," my mother said, "that he has played us for fools. But everybody knows," she said, now turning to look me in the eye, "that it's the fools who always get the gold in the end."

I was about to drop a ribbon on her head but her beady, angry eyes made me stop. Instinctively, I pocketed the plastic sleeve containing my gold.

For the remainder of Christmas day, I was stuck in my room with Barry Manilow. My Burl Ives and *Charlie Brown Christmas* albums had been confiscated. I had been stripped of Christmas.

I hadn't minded so much giving up the walkie-talkies, the candy, or even the LED watch.

It had been the gold that hurt, physically, to part with.

My mother was originally going to let me keep the gold as my only present. Until I smart-mouthed, "*Good,* because it's the only one I wanted anyway."

That's when she pried it from my greedy little fingers and locked me in my room.

It made me so mad I wanted to scream and pound my fists against the hollow-core door. Christmas was in shambles. I supposed I was partially to blame. Or perhaps all to blame.

And the more I thought about it, the more horrible it seemed I had behaved.

And then I went from feeling mad to sorry.

I was released for dinner. My mother had made a ham with cloves on top just the way I liked, except I didn't get to stick any of the cloves into the top of the ham myself, which was my favorite thing in the world.

When I looked up, she was already looking at me. And she was on the verge of smiling. She held out two fists. "Pick a hand," she said. I looked from her eyes to her fists, then back at her eyes. There was no clue to be seen in them so I picked the right one.

She extended her hand, rolled the fist over, and uncurled her fingers. A single clove was stuck to the center of her palm.

Happy.

I took the clove and I carefully pressed it into the golden rind of the ham that now sat before me on the platter.

Then she presented me with her other fist and I was surprised.

She waited.

I pointed to the fist.

When she uncurled her fingers, gold was there.

Ask Again Later

*T*HE SUNLIGHT ON the bed was that clean, white light of winter without any tinge of yellow or gold; it was a lensed, glassy light that erased the shadows. So much pure, diffused sun felt like a shoplifted luxury; like sleeping until eleven on a Monday morning. Even without my glasses, I could make out the heavy drapes and see that they were pulled all the way open.

My first thought, *What a spectacular morning*, was followed immediately by, *But I don't have drapes.*

Even out of focus, a seven-foot armoire was difficult to miss, especially when it was exactly where my beer-can pyramid should have been.

I blinked.

A marble-topped nightstand was on my left. Once again, *Where was my upside-down white plastic laundry hamper bedside table?* The only marble in my apartment was the threshold at the bathroom door.

There was a delicate, pale green china cup and saucer on top of the nightstand. The cup was half-filled with coffee and two spent Sweet'N Low packets lay on the marble beside the saucer.

The handle of the cup faced away from me, and though I noticed this, I did not consider what it implied.

Beyond these few details, I could not see. Though, I did believe I could make out a *form* on the . . . *Was it another bed? Right there on the other side of the nightstand.*

One might have reasonably concluded I was not alone in that room.

I had consulted the Magic Eight Ball so frequently as a child, that even at twenty-six, the toy's ominous answers floated to the surface of my internal window, even when I hadn't consciously asked a question. SIGNS POINT TO YES came to mind.

The bedding had the depth of a snowstorm; I felt buried beneath the richest, most sumptuous mounds of fabric, layers of it: sheet, blanket, duvet, bedspread. All of this, too, was foreign.

There could be no doubt: this was not my futon.

It was with a mounting sense of distress that my eyes traveled once again to the window where I saw now that the drapes and the bedding shared the same design.

That is when I knew that something in the universe itself had, indeed, malfunctioned; I was somewhere color-coordinated.

I scanned the nightstand but did not see the familiar glint of gold—a tiny lighthouse flashing: HERE ARE YOUR GLASSES. So I leaned over the edge of the bed and began to spider my hand along the carpeted floor. I'd stepped on enough pairs of glasses to know that mine seemed to prefer the floor.

Blind, and with my head upside down, I glanced toward the foot of the bed and saw a slash of red. *Odd,* I thought. *What could that be?*

And in reply, five words burned through the murky blue of Magic Eight Ball juice: BETTER NOT TELL YOU NOW.

I thought, *Seriously. What is that?*

Finally, my fingers located the glasses tucked into an uncanny little crevice behind the front legs of the nightstand; a spot seemingly designed to attract and retain fallen objects. No human eyes would ever have found them there. I plucked them from the crevice, hoping not to find a bent temple. What I found instead was a pair of lenses so mental-patient filthy and caked with crud, it shocked me that I had been able to see through them. Pretending that that had not been a pubic hair on the left lens but only an exceedingly svelte and limber dust bunny, I fogged the lenses with my breath and attempted to polish them with the edge of the sheet. As I did this, I glanced over at the streak of red and as I stared, more detail was revealed, not unlike a word rising slowly to the surface of my internal Magic Eight Ball.

A band of white *smoke* seemed to surround the red cloud. And there was a luminous, tiny golden star—in the center.

Glasses were amazing.

Because the instant the mysterious floating blob was resolved in clarifying detail, there was no puzzle to what it was. Any kindergarten-aged child in America knew the answer.

The red velveteen, the white fur trim and then the glossy flash of black. Yes, that would be the belt. The sun kicked a highlight off the buckle: *a tiny golden star.*

So. If that's Santa's suit, I wondered dangerously, *where might* Santa *be?*

For the answer, I needed only to slide my eyes left, to the bed on the other side of the nightstand.

He was probably about sixty-five. A portly gentleman, apparently naked beneath the sheet, he had a full, white beard and silver, somewhat stylish reading glasses perched low on his nose. He was peering at me over the top rim of those glasses, with an amused little smile.

If the notepad next to the telephone was correct, I was naked in the bed next to Santa Claus at the Waldorf Astoria in New York City.

There was even a *twinkle* in his eye. "Ah, bonjour!" he said. "Bonjour." He took a noisy sip from the cup of coffee.

I removed my glasses and tossed them on the nightstand. Then I dropped my head into my hands and groaned; undoubtedly rather rude as far as gestures went.

This was not happening to me.

YOU MAY RELY ON IT.

I still felt slightly drunk from the previous night. Of which I could remember absolutely nothing. I did know that a Long Island Iced Tea would have really hit the spot at that moment.

"Aww," he said. "Not feeling so clear-headed this morning?"

When I slipped my glasses back on and looked at him, he raised his eyebrows.

"Oh, no," I assured him. "I feel *extremely* clear-headed

this morning, as a matter of fact. And that's the problem."

Oh.

My.

God.

It was apparent that something terrible had happened. I was at the Waldorf with Santa and I didn't have
even the vaguest idea how the hell this came to be. Was it
possible my glasses were so filthy I could have mistaken
him for a hockey coach?

Given my history, I was most likely at a bar when I saw
a dirty old Frenchman in a ratty Santa suit. That much I
could believe. Something about *December* in New York
always squeezed the crazies out from under their rocks.
It was not uncommon to be having a drink and see a guy
walk in with cute little reindeer antlers clipped to his
head, even a red stocking cap. Rather less common, I
supposed, was an old fat guy in a full Santa suit, though
that was beside the point.

My question was: How did I go from merely *seeing* the
dirty French Santa in a bar to being in his hotel room the
next morning? And this presented me with an actual
equation. How did one plus one equal old French Santa?

I was accustomed to waking up in bed with somebody
I had never seen before. Not, however, with a man *in costume*; one old enough to be dead from natural causes.

This was a new low for even me, a person who was essentially the gold medalist in the category.

I climbed out of bed because, no matter what, it was better to be dressed. This much was perfectly clear.

I saw my clothes, neatly folded on the low upholstered bench at the foot of my bed. As I stepped into my boxer-briefs, Santa said, "Mmm, even nicer by the light of day."

Horrified, I looked up to see him stripping the covers away from his own doughy body, revealing a small, World War II–era erection. A leering, oily smile had formed on his lips.

He patted the unoccupied side of his mattress. "Come over here, Kevin," he said, "and get your tail back into my bed."

I froze, one leg in my jeans, the other raised. So, I was Kevin. Which was fine. It showed I'd had the good sense not to supply him with my actual name. So why had I followed him here in my actual body?

And what was this business about my tail? He'd said to get my tail *back* into his bed, which implied that I, Kevin, had been *in* his bed at an earlier point in time.

Dirty French Santa's greedy little finger-eyes were trained on my crotch; I yanked the jeans up and buttoned them, zipping the fly with a finality that I hoped suggested a door slam. I stretched my T-shirt over my head, jabbed my arms through the holes and yanked it down. I felt the tag scratch at my throat but didn't want to take the time to turn it around.

Fiddling with his irritating little doodad, he asked, "What makes you so shy all of a sudden? Hmm? Maybe you need another massage, yes?"

It was interesting, I noted, how the brain seemed to actually perceive a *slowing* of time when one was faced with unspeakable horror.

I tried to mask the panic in my voice by raising the volume, which only made me sound hysterical. *"You need to tell me exactly what happened in this appalling room last night."*

Santa was enjoying this. He cackled and produced a wad of phlegm, which led to a coughing fit. He covered his mouth with his plump, pale little fist and cycled through his repertoire of deeply repulsive sounds, gasping for air between gags, as he tried to expel what I could only assume was a dead rat. *"Excuse me,"* he said, finally. "I had a little something stuck in my throat." He waited a beat before adding, "But not what I *wish* was stuck in my throat!" His watery eyes were now bloodshot.

I winced. What a hideous creature; ebola in need of a back wax.

"As for last night," he continued in his slippery eel of a voice, "oh, but I wouldn't even know *where* to begin.

84

You were a very naughty, naughty boy." He wagged his finger at me and then made a small French clucking sound, like he was attempting to nurse at the tit of a barn cat.

I stared down at him, wanting to cut his dark tongue right out of his foul mouth.

"Yeah, okay, okay, that's cute. And you would of course know that I was 'naughty' because you, after all, are Santa Claus. Ha. I get it." I bored into him with my most leveling gaze. My jaw muscles clenched and unclenched. "Now, what I'd like to know is, what happened during this little massage of yours? Do I need to be worried about catching dirty French Santa pox?"

Haughty and defensive now, he threw his hands up and shrugged. "What could we do? You were drunk. *You couldn't even get an erection,* that's how drunk you were."

I narrowed my eyes, on the brink of pointing out it was *possible* that alcohol was not the only contributing factor to my impotence.

But then, I couldn't do that, because apparently I had come here *willingly.* As in, *by choice.* As in, *"Yeah, the repulsive slob in the nubby Santa outfit—over there, the French one propping himself up against the piano, snapping his fingers out of time, that's the one.* Of course *I'm sure, Wrap him up!"*

Santa then said, "Besides, you just wanted more,

more, more of that Kahlúa," with an exaggerated frown of disgust on his face.

Okay, enough was enough.

I was drinking *Kahlúa*?

This was more alarming than waking up naked with Santa.

The only time it was okay to drink Kahlúa was if you were thirteen, your parents were out of town, and you needed something to break the ice so you could have sex with your homeroom teacher. Kahlúa was medicine for teenagers; not a drink for grown-ups.

"Well, thanks for keeping it top shelf," I muttered.

The French fucker looked quite pleased with himself, but at least he'd draped the sheet over the more offensive regions of his body.

I said, "The only other thing is, are you *absolutely fucking positive* nothing happened," and I nearly wept finishing the sentence, "between us?"

The nasty old thing looked at me as if I had accused him of lifting fifty bucks from my wallet. Which, now that I thought of it, I should inspect.

He started yammering at me in French. I'd never learned French because, even though it pisses the French off, they will speak English eventually.

I waved my hands like a traffic cop. "Whoa, whoa,

whoa, hold on *Monsieur Santa,* no more of the romance language while I'm in the room, okay? Let's try it again in the nice, universal *English.*"

His face was red with indignation. *"Comment osez-vous, vous vingt francs pute?"* he spat. "I did *not* take advantage of you. *You said I could.* You said, *'I don't care, do whatever.'* Those were your precise words."

It was better when he was speaking French and I didn't know what he was saying.

"Um, okay. So. What, exactly, did you do?" I tried to make this sound friendly and nonaccusatory but it came out bouncy yet maniacal. Like Mr. Rogers opening up his vest to reveal his torso strapped with explosives.

Dirty French Santa looked kind of pissed, to be honest. He had folded his hairy sausage-arms across his chest and was pouting. I wanted to repeatedly slam his face into the toile headboard.

Instead, I smiled at him and nodded encouragingly.

Still pouting and with his bottom lip protruding like a five-year-old's, he admitted, "I put hair conditioner from the bathroom on your back. And I rub. *That is all.*"

I was going to throw up in my mouth.

I took a deep breath. *However.*

It could have been worse. A lot worse. So in a very sad and ugly way, this was great news. Technically? I had not been *defiled* by Santa. And this was a huge accomplishment for me, given the circumstances. It was, incredibly, something I could be proud of.

Relieved, I smiled at the sad old sack of mess, which seemed to *inflate* something within him.

He added, "And as I was rubbing, you kept shouting, *'Fuck me, Fuck me Santa. I want to go blind. Make me blind!'* "

There had been many instances throughout my life when I felt I had actually earned an Academy Award, but there had been nobody there to witness the obvious triumph of my performance. My smile did not falter, and I continued to look at him with sincere kindness. Though how I wished for a handgun.

Finally, I said, "Now, Santa, that isn't true and you know it." I *no-no-no*'ed my index finger at him. "Naughty, naughty old man. It's not nice to make up stories."

That *really* pissed him off.

"How dare you accuse me of lying?" he roared as he removed his reading glasses. "I am a member of *Le Conseil de Prud'Homme*s. I will not be insulted by an American alcoholic with garbage of the brain."

I slowly raised only my left eyebrow while lifting just the right corner of my mouth to form an asymmetrical smile; a wise-ass smirk. As a child, I had spent hours practicing this special effect of the face. At that moment, as I was about to get the hell out of that unfortunate room and its fat, pitiful circumstances, it paid off.

"You know, American alcoholics are pretty fucking hard to insult. You are talking to somebody who drank too much *Kahlúa* last night, which is not exactly a 1983 Château Margaux. So, as we say over here, calm the motherfuck down."

When his petulance had subsided, I gently asked the question that made me wish for death. "I just want to confirm—and I *will* take your word for it—did you, then, *fuck me blind?*"

"I slipped it in once and that's all," he said, his head straight forward, looking at the wall instead of me. An infuriating *dignity* attempted to cling to his doughy features.

The world became a very bad place.

"What?" I shouted.

And now he looked at me. He pounded his fists on the mattress in frustration or perhaps humiliation. "I told you, I slip it in *once*. Then out. And then," he stopped, catching himself.

With only my eyes, I made him know that I would saw off his head if he didn't tell me the rest.

He held his face up, elevated his chin. That revolting *pride* thing again. "And then *frottage* on the back.

89

Just a little slide-against. Then I come, I wipe off. That's it. Everybody happy."

I was now standing directly beside him, looming over him in precisely the position one would assume if one were holding a large rock and intended to crush another person, say Santa Claus. "Oh no, no, no. Everybody *not* happy," I shouted. "This is *not* me happy. I am not happy."

I pointed my finger at him. "Are you absolutely *sure* you have told me everything?

Santa looked up at me, right in the eyes. "I have told you the truth."

Miserably, I knew he had.

That meant, I needed medical assistance immediately: I needed a brain transplant.

The next week, a series of blood tests ensued. When the doctor told me I was fine, I asked him, "What else can you test for? I want you to test for everything French. And everything old-person. Whatever parasites or gangrenes they get, test for those, too." I shuddered. "What about gout? Is that communicable?"

But even if my blood was clean, my mind was now

contaminated. While I didn't remember the Foulness, I remembered the Fouler.

Over and over I replayed that horrible morning. From waking up in the sun-drenched room and seeing the hazy red blur, right up to the point where I stood above him wishing I had a hefty river stone.

That awful voice of his. Those sneaky, cloudy eyes. The liver spots. I knew I shouldn't continue to obsess over what had happened. But it was my own internal car accident: I had to keep rubbernecking no matter how grisly because there was always a chance I'd see a head roll past.

I nearly called the doctor back to schedule a medical memory wipe, something where a full day is removed, along with maybe the two or three surrounding days just to make sure. But I knew I simply had to force myself to stop dwelling on and thus polishing the horror of what happened to a blinding sheen. Down the *I-did-it-with-Santa* road there was only madness.

Rather, I had to think of the entire experience like an incredibly high state income tax bill or Beanie Babies—an unpleasant reality, now in the past.

I'd forgotten plenty of guys before, I could do it again.

Or so I believed for about thirty seconds. Right up until I was passing a magazine store and glanced in the

91

window. There he was: *my lover.* Three of him, actually—three paper Santa heads taped to the window.

This was only the second week in December. I would be seeing an awful lot of Santa over the coming days. And then there was next year to look forward to. And the year after that. And every year for the rest of my life.

Most everybody had made at least one bad, drunken decision in their lives. Called an ex at two in the morning. Or perhaps had a little too much to drink on a second date and wept inconsolably while revealing how simply *damaged* one was, while nonetheless retaining an uncommonly large capacity for love. That kind of thing was, while regrettable, at least comprehensible.

But waking up with someone generationally inappropriate, like your grandfather's best buddy?

Obviously I needed to do my best to forget what Santa and I had shared.

And to hope he died soon.

The problem was, my grandfather's best buddy was more famous than Coca-Cola. And he was eternal.

This was really bothering me: I picked up that sad crusty thing in a bar. He didn't fall from a sleigh in the sky. I wasn't bound and gagged and brought to him, a gun at my temple.

I selected him.

So, was this some appalling repressed fetish? Something, God help me, unleashed after I had a few drinks in me? Had that ubiquitous holiday image somehow woven its way through childhood and into my psychosexual development, only to be expressed in early adulthood, under conditions made ideal by the consumption of too much alcohol?

Somehow, *that* did not seem fixable.

If one was sexually attracted to Santa, one had departed from mainstream reality. This was no different from turning down dates and staying home weekends because *you were saving yourself for Cap'n Crunch.*

OUTLOOK NOT SO GOOD.

I decided to execute a small amount of forensic work on my sexual history. I needed to sit down and analyze The Guy List. This was a list I'd started shortly after moving to Manhattan. On it, I'd scribbled the name or some identifying characteristic of every guy I'd ever had sex with.

I had defined *sex* as: *seeing them naked while they are under the impression there will soon be sex.* Because many times, there was no sex. Sometimes, I got grossed out and left. Other times, I was so drunk I got lost in their bathroom. And then sometimes, they broke the spell by speaking and becoming an actual person, which made any kind of intimacy impossible.

I would analyze previous sexual partners and see if I could uncover a possible virus of attraction. Retrace my steps to try and identify any behavioral patterns that could explain how I ended up bedding an old guy with a fat suit.

Neil Bookman

The Unfortunate One

Battery Park City Ick

Saab Man

Jukebox Man

Penthouse Nut with Football

Park Avenue Poor Baby

Hell's Kitchen Actor

Akita Wednesday

Investment Banker Slime

Auggie's Pizza Boy

Calvin Klein Model

Stairway Man

Chef of the Village
San Francisco Beard
Chicago Door Unlock
Ad Asshole Dude
Barstool Man Chicago
Head Too Small
Camping Dad
Mr. Boston
Pier Guido
Garage Man
Dr. Little Dick
Teacher Man from Brooklyn
Jay Leno Mouth
Ricky Ricardo
Piano Actor (falsetto laugh)
Something Wrong Down There Guy
Traveling Investment Banker
Egyptian Hunk Doc
Pilot (anatomically incorrect)
Breath Deformity
Porkpie Hat East Village Fuckwad
German Music Teacher Guy
Cocaine Guy from NYU

Looking at the list, I was surprised that a phrase like *Breath Deformity* could recall the man so vividly.

Breath Deformity was actually a real catch of a guy. He had dark hair and he was ruggedly handsome, some sort of durable Mediterranean stock. He owned an optics company so he was loaded. And his apartment was just amazingly cool—the kind of place you see in a magazine and think, *No real person lives there.*

But the breath.

It wasn't like you could ever sit him down and tell him he had a problem and should see a dentist. This kind of breath couldn't be fixed; it was a birthmark. It was an extra finger. It was simply a part of him. What he needed was somebody who had been in a car accident and suffered the loss of their olfactory bulb.

The Calvin Klein model just fell into my lap; I hadn't pursued him. For some reason, he'd come after me. It didn't make sense, a man of such physical beauty actively pursuing an alcoholic with deep-set eyes and rashy skin. I was doubtful that he really was a Calvin Klein model, actually. Until he took me to Times Square and showed me his billboard.

I hadn't been interested in him, I realized, because he had been so interested in me. It was suspicious.

Ricky Ricardo, I'd liked. He didn't return my calls. And this had made me insane with frustration because I was convinced I could make him like me.

I realized suddenly, there was a chilling commonality among the men. With the exception of the first, I had been less than sober with all of them.

As I had expected, over the following days I ran into Santa all over town, and each time it made me cringe. The vast quantity of images—photographs, illustrations, molded plastic figures, stuffed and life-size—was literally everywhere. The worst were the ones ringing bells and clutching little red charity pails. The glossy black boots, the geographical location of a street corner, the sweat clinging to the dense eyebrows on Santa's face, and the wad of one-dollar bills lent these Santas the gritty, *available* sheen of prostitutes.

But no matter what kind of Santa I saw, to me he always looked like a leering, glassy-eyed old Frenchman, overheating inside his costume, desperate to rub his dangly bits on any drunk's lower back.

Then something happened that I didn't expect. In fact, it never so much as crossed my mind that such a possibility even existed: I saw my Santa again.

I was walking through the West Village to get to the East. As I passed what I had always considered the sleaziest and most depressing bar in Manhattan, there was

Santa—sitting in the window at a stool, with a beer in one hand and a cigarette in the other.

He was wearing his rat-fur-trimmed hat.

If I had ever seen a sadder, more dejected specimen of a human person, I could not remember it. There was no twinkle in his eyes, none of that dignity I'd seen him cling to back at the hotel. That irritating spark of *French-ness* was gone from him.

Ruination. That's what I saw. And it made me sick; it made me ache.

I felt a pull; powerful and impossible to oppose—moon versus sea.

I wanted to comfort him and fix him. I wanted to do something to remove his terrible hollow.

And I didn't know, maybe this was how he had looked on the night I'd met him. Maybe I'd seen him and felt the same thing I felt now. Maybe this need to repair the broken man was a problem of mine. Maybe it was what therapists called "an issue."

The truth was, I didn't care. It didn't matter.

I was going in there and I was going to sit beside him. And I was going to keep him company.

I would make him laugh.

We would drink *Kahlúa.*

I would ask him how to say *I'm sorry* in French.

Later, I would leave and walk home to my apartment. And he, I assumed, would climb into his sleigh and ride off into the black, black night.

IT IS DECIDEDLY SO.

Why Do You Reward
Me Thus?

*F*OUR CALLING BIRDS? Three French hens? Two turtle doves? What are turtle doves and why would anybody want one of them, let alone two? And a *partridge* in a *pear tree*? Where the *fuck* was this person shopping?"

Matt said, "You know, Burr, it's actually *inspiring* to be around you, you're so filled with the holiday spirit. Has anybody ever told you that you should be a father? *I didn't think so.*"

"I'm just saying. It's a stupid song. And I can promise you, not one American born after the Dust Bowl has even the slightest idea what it's about. Yet we all know it. We all sing it. Then we teach it to our brats and they run around singing it all year.

"And what's the message? Did you ever notice that a lot of the alleged 'gifts' happen to be *people?* Eight maids a-milking, so that's prepubescent girls forced into labor, probably inserting the underwire in bras. And then nine ladies dancing? That's the sex trade. I won't even go into the five golden rings. But *somebody's* paying somebody off for something.

"Human trafficking and birds? That's a good Christmas song? Oh, and swans, which are the drunk, violent ex-boyfriends of the bird world. Because what would any holiday be without a little domestic violence?"

I threw a stick of salami into the hand basket.

Matt said, "You sure you want that? Seems like you've already got one of those crammed pretty far up your ass."

"I *do not* have a stick up my ass, you gay sack of cat shit. I just resent the mindlessness of it all. And our obedience. Every year just after *Halloween*—I mean, they should at least wait for Thanksgiving—we're supposed to join hands and walk together into the Holiday Spirit. It's like a fire drill at the office."

Matt said, "Yeah, of course. It's *exactly* like a fire drill. I *totally* see where you're going with this."

"But it's true. There you are, finally getting some real work done. And all of a sudden, your head is sawed in half by this atrocious *blast.* You don't even know what

102

it is; it just stuns you like a brain-wasp. But then you get it and so you figure, *Oh, well this doesn't apply to me. It's for the other people, on the lower floors.*"

Matt kind of smirked, but more in an I-can't-believe-you're-allowed-to-live way than anything else.

"But guess what," I continued. "The fat fuck of a fire warden—who has apparently worked in your office for like forty years even though you've never once seen his particular brand of ugly—is right now on your floor barking orders and telling you that, oh yes, this fire drill *does* motherfucking apply to you. And you will leave the building right this minute, so get up and get moving, *buddy.*"

"Yeah, and this ties into Christmas how, exactly?"

"Because," I said, annoyed, "it's forced on you. It's mandatory participation even if you have better things to do. Higher-floor things."

"Oh," he said, making a face like I'd just puked on his Gucci loafers. "Somebody seriously needs to take you out behind the barn and shoot you between the ears. *Higher-floor things.* God help us all if you ever get elected to power."

"Well you can be sure I'd stop forcing the poor Jews to tart up their humble little temple dedication anniversary into some corn-fed whore of a holiday to compete with our super-slut, three-titted Christmas."

"Now I don't even know what language you're speaking, let alone what you're yammering on about."

"*Hanukkah,*" I said, annoyed that he was so slow, mentally. Probably due to his odious career in *managed care.* "Hanukkah is only supposed to be a minor holiday for the Jews. It marks the date that one of their temples was dedicated. Or rebuilt. Or rededicated. Or taken back from Palestinian Pizza Palace and turned back into a Jewish temple. Whatever. But it's *real estate* based. Not *father-of-all-mankind* based, as corrupted by the Coca-Cola icon in the red fat suit. But we make them make a huge deal out of it because guess what? That's what drug addicts do. Nobody likes to shoot up alone. The more the merrier."

"Okay," he said. "I think maybe you need some *alone time.* Why don't we get back in touch *after* the holidays? Like a year after." And before I could helpfully inform him that the average survival time with stage 4 melanoma in the lung was just a few months, he was gone.

I set my hand basket down next to the peanut butter and left the store. I hated shopping and only did it when I was with other people because it made me seem more normal. "Come with me to the store?" sounded way less freakish than "Come sit with me in the dark while I drink alone?"

But I didn't even know why I bothered. I was horrible

at this *friends* thing. I said all the wrong things except when I was busy saying all the mean ones. And in the end, I hated everybody and everything.

Outside on Seventh Avenue, the sun irritated my eyes. The winter light in New York seemed somehow sharper than the summer light. It was bluer, more finely honed.

God, I thought, *I hate the sun.*

I knew what I had become. I wasn't trying to kid myself or anything. I was that old man on the cartoons I used to watch as a kid. What was his name? With the big nose and the ghosts? And there was a little gimp kid that trailed him around? Scrooge, that was it.

And didn't he talk to himself, too?

Actually, there was a clinical term for what I had become: *miserable fuck.*

If you have to be single and you have to be bitter and you also have to be without family for the holidays, Manhattan is the only place to be. And praise Jesus for the Jews, the Chinese, and the alcoholics. If it weren't for them, I wouldn't be able to have sex, eat, or forget all the people I'd had sex with.

As I turned onto Twelfth Street I thought, *But that's what's so great about New York. All these people exist here and they don't give a shit about Christmas, either.*

Let the Upper East Side bitches drag their oily hedgehog hedge fund husbands from party to party. I will get drunk and have sex with the Jews. I will order General Tso's chicken.

While I sip my Rolling Rock, all the little sheep-shoppers will race from one store to another and pass out five dollar bills to the bums. Which really should be against the law, like feeding the pigeons.

It was as if an infection, an actual virus, swept the nation once a year.

Fortunately, my brittle exterior provided immunity. And as I reached my apartment building I thought, *Why?* Why go upstairs when I could get a head start on Christmas and reverse my awful current state of sobriety. It was, after all, less than forty-eight hours away. That's only a couple of bars in alcoholic time. Which was like dog years, except without the fleas.

I had a mice-in-the-oven kind of life. I might as well turn on the gas.

Even at the filthiest hole-in-the-wall bar down by the West Side Highway they were playing "Jingle Bells," "Rudolph the Red-Nosed Reindeer," "Here Comes Santa Claus" and my own favorite, "The Chipmunk Song," which made you glad arsenic was invented. And all of this joyous noise was playing on an endless loop. Satan himself was the Christmas DJ.

Truly, this was music with no prefrontal cortex.

So if you sat and drank enough Rolling Rocks, the same songs repeated over and over. And if you rolled your eyes and muttered, "Jesus fucking Christ," within hearing range of the bartender, he might walk right up to you and say, "What's the matter, fella, didn't get to sit on Santa's lap today at Macy's?"

The fact is, if you don't "get into the holiday spirit" people will not only be angry with you, they will think something is wrong with you and they will decide you are a bad person. A spoil sport. "He's a Grinch."

They will feel a visceral mistrust, a hatred, even.

They will reject you.

And you will find yourself on the outside of the snow globe.

I paid up and walked out.

What seemed like a couple of hours later, I suddenly sort of *woke up* I guess and found myself sitting on the filthy red carpeting outside the entrance to the Art Greenwich Twin at the top of my street. My back was pressed against the glass door to the lobby. And when I glanced down, I saw that my clothes—khakis, white T-shirt, blue button-down shirt, Timberland boots—everything I had on was inexplicably dirty. Almost as if I had been wearing the exact same outfit for days and done nothing but slime around on the streets. And I was smoking a cigarette.

But none of that truly alarmed me. The jolt of terror arrived because there were two reeking, shockingly filthy wretches huddled up next to me, one on either side. Call them whatever you wish—*the homeless, bums, vagrants, winos, bag men, beggars, hobos, tramps*—but when your nose was literally inches away from their hair? The only name that fit was *disgusting.*

I walked past this theater every evening, usually looking in the opposite direction because after the last show let out, these very bums arrived. They came with their cardboard boxes and stolen shopping carts piled high with debris and filth. And right there where I was now sitting—on the pitiful threadbare red carpeting in front of the doors to the movie theater—they set up a little camp.

It absolutely *stunned* me the city didn't come along with fire hoses and just wash them out of here. They were like Norway rats, just an ugly part of the city that had to be endured if you wanted the good parts. But just because you had to step on a few rats on the way to work every day didn't mean you had to bend over and hand them some Roquefort. So I never paid any attention to the creatures.

Yet. There I was. Right in the heart of their clan. And here's the really weird thing: according to my watch, it was 3:00 A.M. On Christmas morning. Which kind of begged the question, *Where did I put those forty hours I was carrying around with me?*

I remembered the bar. I remembered "The Chipmunk Song." I remembered "The Chipmunk Song," *again*. I even remembered it a third time.

But after that, it was all a little fuzzy. My memories were not quite as sharp. *Blurry*, was maybe the word. Blurry or completely missing. *That* was it, right there.

At least they hadn't ripped my coat off me, I thought. Not that it did much good. It must have been twenty degrees. These bums were nuts to be camping outside in this weather.

God, what was I doing thinking about the weather? I had to get up, pry myself out from between those horrible creatures. And as I moved about two inches forward, it was instantly apparent that it was not my coat which was keeping me warm: it was the bums.

A more sickening feeling I cannot imagine. But the stinking heat radiating from those two life-forms was the only thing keeping me alive. Of course, now that I thought about it, I could actually cross the street and go home. I didn't have to stay here one more minute.

I began to stand up.

Just flexing the muscles in my arms to push myself up was enough; the movement caused both of the bums to spring fully awake and launch to their feet. They were standing above me in less time than it had taken for me to even get my ass off the ground.

Seeing me, their faces instantly relaxed into easy, friendly smiles. Relief, even. "Oh, hey, man. You scared the shit out of me. I felt that movement down by my feet and I thought somebody was trying to take my shoes," the bum said, then he laughed. He was a white bum, only around thirty. So that was pretty scary, the guy was just five years older than me.

The other guy was a black bum and he wasn't all that old, either, now that I got a good look at him. He might even have been the younger of the bums. "Are you okay?" he suddenly asked me. "To be honest, some of us have

110

been a little worried about you. I was keeping an eye on you myself—Shirley asked me to, but I would have anyway." He smiled. "Wanted to make sure you didn't choke to death or swallow your cigarette." Then he said, "Oh, and ah, thanks again for the sandwiches. I'm not sure it registered the first time I told you," and he chuckled and reached forward, slapping me on the shoulder.

Was I among bums or frat boys? And who the fuck was Shirley?

A third bum meandered over. This one was a little more fucked up. I mean, they were all fucked up. But the first two, there was something a little clean about them on the inside. They almost seemed like regular people. Or like they had been regular people not too long ago. But this new third one, his eyes were holes; he looked nasty and hollow inside.

He handed me a beer. " 'Ere ya go," he said.

But I liked the guy.

Sometimes, that rough-around-the-edges look in a person's eyes was really just good manners combined with an uncomfortable mattress.

"Man, oh man," he said, "you are one crazy motherfucker." He started to laugh and looked at the other two bums to join in. They kind of smiled but didn't really laugh. And then the crazy, beer-giving bum asked, "So man, what's up with you? Like, all of a sudden you swoop down on us like you're Batman or something and you dump all these sandwiches and beer and cash from the ATM machine on us. Fucking nuts!"

I thought, *I'll say it's nuts.* Jesus. I did that? How *much* beer?

He laughed some more and it was that laugh where the tongue is kind of fat and forward in the mouth and there's a dopey smile. And it all just lets you know that this is not a really smart person. So proceed with caution.

"Dude, do you even remember anything? Like, do you remember talking to Boner? That was fucking hysterical—hiss-ter-i-cal! What was that shit you was talking about, Boner? Semi-exotics or something?"

The black guy said, "Semiotics, ChapStick. We were discussing my former life as a semiotics major at Brown." He glanced at me. "Do you recall any of our conversations?"

I caught the plural. "Um, actually? I really kind of don't remember a whole lot. Jesus, it's freezing out here. How can you guys—" And I stopped myself.

The first bum, though, he answered the part of the question I left off. "It just happens. You don't decide one day: *I think I'll go out and become homeless.* It's a whole set of circumstances that align in just the right way."

And the Chapstick guy said, "Yeah, and smack."

"Yeah, that didn't help."

I was thinking, *What the hell are semiotics?* Is that something I should know about?

Two more came over, girl bums. And all the guys started acting like guys, teasing and fiddling with the girls. And they were all girly, laughing and slapping shoulders and saying, "Screw you," but playfully.

I was trying to think of a way to thank them, then back away and walk across the street to my apartment. But at the same time, there was something so oddly compelling about it all. Like with the girls. The way they both had relatively clean nails and hair. The rest of them, forget it. But these little details—hair and nails. It was like this was their last link to civilization and they weren't going to give it up.

It frightened me in a way I didn't understand.

And they were both *very* drunk.

I wondered if I had appeared as drunk to these bums as those girl bums appeared to me now? Or had I been even drunker?

And was I with them for the whole two days?

One of the drunk bum girls looked at me and said, "Sam-which man? Can you spot me another ten? *Please?*"

And that's when I realized, *Yup. It does appear that I have settled in quite well with these nomads.*

And suddenly, it made a kind of perverse sense. It

was, after all, my greatest fear: *I would end up a bum, like one of them. A nothing.* I didn't have family to fall back on. It was all up to me. I'd been—I wasn't sure if *afraid* was the word (maybe *angry??*)—with bums my whole life. I'd never seen them as actual people. But on some level, didn't I have to know they were?

I must have developed some grand notion when I was drinking: *Let us study the bums!* Maybe thinking that doing so would prevent me from becoming one. Even though I knew I of course couldn't *actually* ever be a bum. I had ambitions and, I thought, *some* kind of talent. I wasn't lazy like the bums. Though this thought didn't comfort me as much as I expected it would.

God, it was all so Phil Donahue. And why did my mind keep flashing on an image of a hand extending a wad of tissues, clean and white: an offering.

Did I friggin' *cry* with the bums? I did, didn't I?

Man.

Despite evidence to the contrary, I hated drinking to the point that I misplaced really big slabs of time. And then slowly, over hours, days, weeks, or even months, recalling with horror what I did or said while in such a lubricated state. It was like I was two people—or more. And I didn't personally know any of them.

Just then, a tall and elegant black woman approached. At first I thought she was in evening wear; a dark pantsuit and a long coat. But as she neared me I could see that her clothes were old, the dark colors not quite matching, and the coat was a man's cut. Everything was well-worn, though meticulously cared for.

I was sitting back down with my new friends, who didn't seem to know that I lived across the street. I was freezing my ass off but I couldn't leave because it was too fascinating to hear them talk about the crazy guy who descended upon them two days before.

The woman stood above me, then reached down and extended her smooth, bony hand. She said, "Augusten, come. Let's take a walk."

She knew my name.

I stood.

What was interesting was that *all* of the others stood, too. Even the girls, and they could barely stand.

She smiled at them and then she led me away. After we were about a block from the cinema, an amused smile formed on her lips. "Do you remember me at all?"

"Sorry," I told her, "I don't."

She laughed. "That's okay. I'm Shirley." And then she told me that we'd sat together on a bench for four hours last night at Abingdon Square Park, just over on Hudson and Eighth. She said we talked. And then we sang some songs to keep warm.

"But I don't sing," I told her.

She smiled. "Yes. *I know.* But I do."

"You're a singer?" I probably had my eyebrows raised because I was thinking, *When? Between Dumpster dives?*

"We had this exact same conversation last night. And you asked me, *'You sing? When, between Dumpsters?'*"

I was horrified. *"I said that?"*

She nodded, then she laughed and put her hand on my shoulder. "It's okay, honey. *Really.* I get it. I do. Like I told you last night, I wasn't *born* out here. I had a real and proper home once. But the booze," she said, her voice trailing off.

"Is that what happened?"

She looked at me. "It isn't the half of what happened, but yeah. Heroin happened, too, and then nothing else after it. I lost my job, my kids. I lost my career. Shit, I was only *twenty-three,* right around your age. And I was thinking, really seriously thinking, about becoming a professional singer."

"Sing something," I said to her. We had just turned left and were, to my surprise, approaching Abingdon Square Park once again. But it was the first time for me. Well, *this* me.

Shirley stared straight ahead, the most curious, almost *knowing*, smile on her face. And her skin—she had such fine skin, impossibly. She didn't seem like a bum at all. She was a lady. A real lady, not a girl or a woman. But a lady from another era. From a time of hats and stocking seams and steamships and *comportment*.

What the hell was she doing being a bum?

Just then, her features changed and a full-blown smile seemed to light up the area around us. She grabbed my arm excitedly. "Look! Look! It's snowing. It's *Christmas* and it's *snowing*!"

It was. Heavy, wet flakes—fat and white, though stained orange by the street lamps, were just beginning to fall.

She clapped. *"We've made enchantment."*

When I didn't say anything she shot me a glance. "Don't you recognize that line?"

"What line?"

She turned and faced me, her hands on her hips. "Are you telling me you have never seen *A Streetcar Named Desire* by Tennessee Williams?"

"I've heard of him," I said.

When she rolled her eyes her whole head rolled with them. "Oh, Lord have mercy on him, he's just a young nincompoop and with your love and guidance, he will grow out of it."

I grinned stupidly. "Is it a movie?"

She slapped me, not lightly, on the shoulder. She was a very touchy person, that was for sure. "Yes, but it was a play first. You know? People . . . stage . . . audience. A *p-l-a-y*," she spelled. Then, "Promise me something."

We had reached the park. She untied the pretty blue scarf around her neck—it was the only thing she wore that was fresh, new—and used it to dust the bench of snowflakes, my side first. Then she dusted her side and we sat.

"Promise me that you will—every once in a while— watch a movie that was made before you were born. And also that you'll see a play now and then. *Promise me*," she said.

I told her I would.

She smiled, pleased. And then she said, "I would ask you to promise me something else but I know you can't."

I didn't say anything. Maybe because she had already known me for four hours but I didn't know her at all; something felt almost spooky.

She was watching me.

"I would ask you to promise me that you will stop this crazy business about wanting to be *'a bum,'* as you so elegantly put it. It is most certainly not, as you say, *'your destiny.'*

"And I would ask you to stop drinking because *I*

know. I know what alcohol does to a person. Especially an ambitious young person with so many dreams and more talent than she even knows what to do with." She smiled and hugged herself. "Oh, when you are young and you have talent and you know, *you know* in your bones that you are going to go so high and so far."

Then she let go of herself. "Those are the ones booze seems to hunger for the most. And once you are with the drink, *oh,* how it strip-mines the soul. In the end you wind up with nothing at all. And it's like that for everybody. It doesn't matter how rich you are or how poor or how white or how yellow or"—and here she looked down at the sidewalk—"how much of whatever it is you have inside you. It just does not matter. The drink is stronger. It will always win and you won't even know it's trying to until it has."

She paused and closed her eyes, lifted her face to the sky. Almost like she was facing the sun, wanting it to give her that good, clean feeling you get from it. But there was only a street lamp and falling snow. And I watched as flakes smacked her face and melted instantly. And then I realized, it must be the feeling of the snow hitting her face and instantly melting that she enjoyed.

She looked at me then, her face moist. Snowflakes had gathered in her eyelashes and made it appear as though she had been crying. And then I wondered, *has she?*

As much as I wanted to think of her as a homeless, rambling drunk, I could not. Because everything she said almost had the tone of a bell, a certain purity. I thought, then, of the phrase, *It rings true.* And I realized, this is where it comes from; somebody telling you *what is,* and you hear the bell in their voice and know they're right.

I almost couldn't tell if she was giving me advice or telling me my fortune, like they were all mixed up.

She continued, "And if I could, I would ask that you write. You kept saying last night that you had *'whole worlds'* inside of you that you needed to get out. Well, get them out, my dear. Focus on this. On something positive for yourself. And for others. I would ask you to set those worlds free."

I caught myself looking at her clothing. And I realized immediately why I was doing it. I was looking for a way to discount everything she was telling me. Because there was something *too* true in her words. It was frightening in a way and I wasn't sure why.

Or, maybe she really was just a rambling drunk.

Suddenly, she clapped her hands. "Okay, enough heavy. It's snowing. It's Christmas. We both have some fine company. How about a song? Shall I sing you something? It'll be my Christmas present to you."

We were sitting side by side on the bench, and she took both of my hands in hers and placed the entire pile of our hands on her lap. She looked at me with such intensity in those eyes, with *dare*.

I smiled at her. "Yes, please do sing something."

I hoped I wouldn't laugh during her rendition of "Have Yourself a Merry Little Christmas" or whatever it was she had in mind.

God, what if she sings "The Chipmunk Song"? I thought, then bit the inside of my cheek.

But Shirley did not sing any Christmas carols nor did she launch into "The Impossible Dream."

Shirley sang an aria.

It was the music of my early childhood; an opera my mother used to play on summer afternoons. I knew it the way a person can know a smell they cannot name but that transports them to one specific moment of one specific, long-gone day. It felt like opening the door to your childhood room and finding that nothing at all had changed. Her voice was unspeakably magnificent.

Perchè, perchè, Signor,
Ah, perchè me ne rimuneri così?

As she sang, the windows of the brownstone across the street shimmered in reply. Her voice had weakened the molecular bond of glass. It filled the space between the flakes of falling snow and packed the air with beauty.

It was, at once, Christmas in Manhattan.

I cried but I did not make a sound.

When she finished, Shirley bowed her head and was silent for a moment. Without looking up she said, "Vissi d'arte from Puccini's *Tosca*. Do you speak Italian?"

I shook my head.

Shirley smiled at me. "It means, *Why, why, O Lord, why do you reward me thus?*"

"Burr, I gotta say—I'm a little worried about you," Matt said over our table at China Grill. "You're almost—and please, don't take this the wrong way, okay? But you're almost—really, quite nearly—sunny. Should I take this to mean that you had yourself a merry little Christmas after all?"

I smiled. "Actually, I did."

He laughed. "Oh, really? That's great, Burr, that really is. Went home to see the folks, did you? Yeah. Except, didn't you have something of a *Dances with Wolves* childhood? Or maybe it was raised by wolves. Either way, I don't think you went home. And I'm your only friend, so we know you weren't with any human people. I think you crawled into your lair with a few bottles of Wild Turkey, whooped it up making prank calls to the maternity ward at Lenox Hill."

"Well, aren't you the new Steve Martin. But I do need to correct you on a few points. The first being, you are not my only friend. I have a number of friends but none of them have ever met because I compartmentalize. You occupy the compartment that exists to make me feel broad-minded and Societally Conscious— all my other friends are over six feet, like me. You are my short-person friend. If you were Asian or black, we could see each other twice as often. That's why I always turn you down when you ask me if I want to go to a movie.

"Now, if you think I would make prank phone calls to a maternity ward, you just don't know me at all. I have doctor friends, and all it would take is one case of good French wine and any one of them would walk up to maternity and tell one of the mothers that she had better prepare herself, she was going to have a Harlequin baby.

"And finally, I spent Christmas Eve and Christmas

morning with some bums, the ones that hang out at the movie theater around the corner from me. The place with the skanky red carpeting?"

Matt choked on the ice cube he'd been knocking around in his mouth. He crunched down on it and killed the choke. "Are you fucking kidding me? You spent your holiday with homeless people on the street?"

"Yeah," I said feeling very bright-eyed. "With one in particular, Shirley."

"You didn't fuck her, I hope. Christ, Burr, tell me it wasn't some homeless chick that got you to play for the other team."

"No, I didn't fuck her, asshole. We talked."

"You talked. What? For two days?"

"Actually, I think it was three. But I only remember one. Part of one, really. And mostly, just a few hours of the one. Anyway, that doesn't matter. What matters is, it was inspiring. Or wait, maybe that's not the right word."

He was watching me. If I levitated or if smoke began to vent through my ears, it wouldn't have surprised him.

"Okay, she didn't *inspire* me. She showed me something more surprising, more astonishing, and more, just *more beautiful* than I know how to explain. It's like, she could have been huge—Beverly Sills or . . . I don't know their names—but she was *The Met*, she was *Carnegie Hall*; Matt, she made the windows shake in their frames."

He was watching me with his eyebrows raised and a sort of, *And when are you going to start making sense?* expression on his face.

"I know this sounds weird, but here's my point—all of it was wasted. She had—*has*—this epic talent and she's a homeless alcoholic. She's not some big opera singer at the Met. She's a bum lady. With this secret voice. Almost like a prisoner with a ten-carat diamond who can only wear it inside her cell and prance around alone.

"And you know the first thing that came into my mind when she was done singing for me? I thought, if I had been born with a talent that large I never would have started drinking. Almost like having such a huge gift would insulate you or protect you. Because it would feel like you had this destiny. So you didn't have to worry. I wouldn't drink because I had too much talent to drink. And then I kind of looked at Shirley sitting there on that bench and I knew, *Oh yes I would*. And something in me just fucking clicked."

Matt placed his elbows on the table and leaned forward. *"Augusten,"* he said.

Just one word, my name.

But with that one word he told me that he was sorry and that he did love me and that he wished for something else, something lighter for me. A life that weighed much less.

125

And I looked up at him and I loved him in return, for not fully understanding, maybe, but not judging me, either.

"I've never been so fucking scared in my life," I said then. "I always thought I could quit drinking whenever I wanted. Or that I was somehow too smart. Or too something. *Whatever,* alcohol wouldn't ruin me. It couldn't. But man, if you had only heard that voice and seen the *size* of her. You know? She was big. Shirley was huge. And still, she got taken down."

Matt reached across the table and brushed the back of his hand against my cheek, and his eyes became smooth, glassy, and warm.

"She scared the shit out of me. And I don't know if it's going to do any good, I really don't. But I do know that I wasn't scared *before.* Maybe that's good? To be scared?"

"Jesus. Well, maybe. Yeah, I guess it's good to be scared. But shit, this was some kind of Christmas you had for yourself. Although I guess, at least you weren't just sitting in your nest alone, piss-drunk. Maybe hanging with these homeless people really is a kind of progress."

"You ever see that *Streetcar Named Desire?*"

"Of course I've seen *A Streetcar Named Desire.* You're the only one of the gays who hasn't."

"Yeah, well I watched it. And it made me think, maybe one of my problems is, I *never* depend upon the kindness of strangers. I would rather bleed to death on the street than depend on a stranger. But maybe that is a huge fucking mistake. Maybe I need to be more like Blanche. But I didn't get why they lock her up at the end. Just for being kind of a slut?"

"You are some kind of fucked up," he muttered under his breath.

"Short," I mumbled without moving my lips.

"Go to hell," he said.

"I need a drink," I told him.

"Hopeless alcoholic."

"Correction," I said, raising my finger high into the air. "Hope*ful* alcoholic. And that may seem like a small difference to you, but all I have ever needed in life was a *maybe.*"

"Hopeful, then," he said, brightly.

I nodded as the waitress finally approached. "Hopeful."

The Best and Only
Everything

*I*T WAS OUR first Christmas as a family. Me, George, and our tiny new virus, AIDS.

The virus was just a few months old. And we were like typical new parents—up and down all night to pace the floors, *in* with the thermometer, *out* with the thermometer, wondering, "What are we going to be dealing with five years from now?" I certainly wouldn't have imagined *diapers*.

In retrospect, I'm not altogether certain it's accurate to say *we*. Because the virus wasn't mine, it belonged to George. And he wasn't the one pacing the floors all night and sticking a thermometer in his mouth every five minutes.

That was me.

George was actually quite calm and logical. He was being treated by the best doctor and taking the best drugs.

His attitude was, "Let's enjoy the moment."

My attitude was, *I cannot fucking believe you stuck your bare hands in his bloody mouth. There was a box of gloves on the table beside his hospital bed. You, yourself, made sure of it. And why were you the one removing the gauze from his mouth instead of a nurse? None of it makes sense.*

Of course, we'd had this conversation before. Many times. It had become our pair of faded jeans, our sweater with too many fur balls on it. It was comfortable, if ugly.

"Augusten, I have told you again and again, I was crazy. I didn't know what I was doing. I was just very upset and he needed that dressing out of his mouth immediately and I didn't think. Listen, it doesn't matter—we can't ever go back and change that moment."

True. But we could get drunk and forget we'd ever had this conversation. That way, when we had it again in a week, it would be all new to me.

Still, I had to try and be grateful for the little things. It was, after all, this very virus that had brought us together, transformed us from "secret lovers" into "official couple."

George's previous boyfriend had entered into an affair with a lawn-care professional. George didn't have a lawn.

Their relationship had been unraveling for a long time and he was feeling stagnant. George had been thinking of leaving the boyfriend when the lawn-care professional turned out to be HIV-positive, passing the virus to George's boyfriend.

The boyfriend did not handle this news well. He figured, *Well, that's it then. I guess I'll just go ahead and die now.*

George said, "You have to *fight* this. *We* have to."

The boyfriend replied, "Where do the whales go when they die?"

That's when I met him.

At eight minutes after five on February 14, 1989, I reached the landing that overlooked the Winter Garden atrium. I approached the wide, grand staircase leading down. Step by step, mistake by mistake, choice by choice, everything that I had ever done, every right instead of left, had been designed to get me here.

In time, I would come to believe that all along, without my ever knowing, every single time I wondered, *Why?*

the answer had been to carry me down *these steps* on *this day* so that I could reach the one moment upon which all the remaining moments of my life would be based.

But at the time, I only thought that I was walking down some stairs to meet a guy.

I didn't even know his name. A date couldn't have been more blind.

The Rizzoli bookstore within the Winter Garden had been his idea. He would be waiting right in front of the store.

Of course at this time of day the offices would be emptying. And the Winter Garden would be filled with people. Many of them standing around, waiting for somebody at one of the restaurants or bars. Bankers, brokers, lawyers, CFOs, VPs—all of them would be buzzing throughout the space. I didn't know how, exactly, I was supposed to find this one very specific though featureless man.

But there he was, right where he said he'd be. The Winter Garden atrium was a swarm of people; he was the only man I saw.

He was dressed in a charcoal suit with chalk pin-stripes. His back was turned to me because he was looking in the window of the bookstore. He didn't appear to be a man waiting for anyone.

But this was the man. There was something about

the specific tilt of his head. Or perhaps it was how he squared his shoulders. I only knew that the instant I saw him, I recognized that he had been *inevitable*. I headed directly for him.

As I approached his broad back and noted the exquisite drape of the suit I realized, *I don't even know his name. I can't just tap this guy on the shoulder and say, "Are you by any chance waiting for—"*

He surprised me by suddenly turning around to face me. He was smiling and he had a bad haircut. The first words George said to me were these: "I was hoping that was you."

And I realized that he had not been looking in the window of the bookstore, but at my reflection, at me, as I walked toward him.

We spent a little over two hours together that first day we met. Less time than most people spend test-driving a car before buying it. Over drinks he made a toast in Greek, *"To pepromenon phugein adunaton."*

It's impossible to escape from what is destined.

It had been only a couple of hours. But I knew.

I may not have known the *facts* of him; I couldn't have told you his favorite color, his birthday, or how he liked his coffee. I couldn't have said if he was a Republican or a Democrat or whether he was allergic to cats; but I knew the *him* of him.

I also knew that one didn't have a second date with this man and then a third, each time getting to know him a little bit better or seeing another "side" of him.

George was *vertical,* not horizontal. All of him was right there from the first moment. He didn't have "sides"; he had fathoms. If you didn't know him after one date, you *couldn't* know him. In this way, he was a treasure perfectly hidden right before my eyes. He was the wreck of the *Sussex* in my backyard swimming pool.

I could only be truly crazy if I walked away from such a find.

I struggled in my apartment that night, his phone number in my hand. I knew that if I called him, that would be it—my life would change. I had never felt such an irrational thing about a person I'd only just met. But I knew it was true.

My attraction had been immediate and profound. And it had nothing to do with the way he looked. My attraction was to what resided between his lines.

And *attraction* is our most ancient drive, it *is* why we *are.* Attraction is the very point of gravity; timespace itself bends to allow it. It is attraction in its pure form that holds the galaxy together.

Attraction is our glue.

I knew this: there was only one of him in the world.

One hour with him was denser than all the years spent with everybody else I had ever known.

My instincts were not mistaken.

My instincts had been with me as I crawled from the swamp; my brain only showed up later. It was my instinct I would trust. Even if it defied logic.

Especially if it defied common sense. I wanted nothing to do with common.

But extremely rare and precious specialty items often carry an extraordinary price. I knew this, too.

It was reckless and insane to feel this way about a person I didn't even know. My mind was hurling itself against the walls of my skull in protest. But beneath my sternum that night, I felt a kind of wisdom. I very nearly heard advice: *Acceptance, when it comes, arrives in waves: Listen with your chest. You will feel a pendulum swing within you, favoring one direction or another. And that is your answer. The answer is always inside your chest. The right choice weighs more. That's how you know. It causes you to lean in its direction.*

I thought, *I don't know who he is, but I know he is mine.*

George picked up before the first ring was out. "I knew you'd call," he said, his voice low, not quite a whisper but a hush.

The hush in his voice. I knew it all right then: the boyfriend, ten feet away. George, sitting by the phone hoping I would call. Hearing the phone and knowing it was me. Hearing my voice and knowing he'd been right. Realizing he was hearing my voice *because* he had been *discovered, he had been seen.* This fact sinking in. This fact sinking all the way in.

Casually, I said, "I liked seeing you."

With the exaggerated singsong inflection of a cartoon character, he said, "I *don't* know what it is . . . *but* it's mine!"

I almost laughed and then I almost sobbed.

Neither of us was expecting what eventually happened. It was very much like a car accident in this respect. You can go over it a thousand times to prove it shouldn't have happened, but it did and it changed everything.

It was certainly not my idea of a romantic situation. But I had loved George approximately twelve minutes after we met. It had not been possible for me to walk away from him. And once I met the boyfriend and saw how loyally and carefully George cared for him, I loved George even more.

I pictured myself in the boyfriend's position, except with a cold. And George bringing me a tuna melt he'd made beneath the broiler, on top of a piece of aluminum foil. Instead of a suction wand.

I did feel filthy, being the secret lover. Invited into the home as a new friend. But the boyfriend didn't seem threatened in the slightest. In fact, he seemed relieved to have George occupied and stop nagging him to *fight this thing.* Often the boyfriend would say, "You two boys go out to a movie. I just want to rest." And I would think, *Would you please just die so we don't have to go out into the cold?* And then I would try and "unthink" the thought by saying in my mind, *That was just a very dark*

137

joke. My way of trying to hold it together. I didn't mean it. Although in truth, I kind of did. By this point, George and I were a couple, in all but name.

Only as the boyfriend was nearing death and whispered to me, "You want him? You can *have* him," did I realize he'd known all along.

I disgusted myself. I stood and watched that man's chest rise with his very last breath and never deflate. And then I left the hospital with his boyfriend. Oh yes, I did.

For the next year, George was in mourning. Pictures of the boyfriend were installed on all surfaces of the apartment and the same somber, funereal George Michael and Enya CDs were played endlessly on the stereo. It seemed there was nothing I could do to reach him. Each morning when I woke up in what was now our bed, the first thing I saw was the photograph of George and his boyfriend beside me on the bedside table.

The boyfriend himself, in ash form, was in an urn atop the mantel.

After a year, when George still refused to let me in, I left him.

And it was only a few months later that a brand-new George drove downtown to my apartment in Battery Park City and rang me from a payphone. The dead boyfriend was no longer *right there* between us. Something else was.

George had tested positive for HIV. It was the same strain that had killed the boyfriend. And according to George, they had never had unprotected sex. And in the last years, no sex at all.

That meant, the day I walked into the boyfriend's hospital room after work and saw George with his bare hands inside his boyfriend's mouth, removing packing gauze from the recent wisdom tooth extraction, was indeed the day he had become infected.

As soon as I walked in I had grasped the magnitude of the scene before me. I shouted at him, "*What* are you doing?" and I pulled him by the arm over to the sink— he still hadn't taken off his suit jacket—where I forced his hands under the faucet at full strength.

After he managed to wash away all the blood, he held up his dripping clean hands to inspect them. George was a nail biter. And the evidence was right there before us: cuts on his thumbs, tears in the flesh beneath the nail of his index and middle fingers. Cuticles ripped. Open wounds. All I could say was, "*Jesus Christ.*"

After six, seven, then eight months with no news, I had come to believe that in a moment of madness, we had experienced a very close call.

Now, as I listened to him describe how the doctor revealed he had seroconverted, I sat in the passenger seat and stared at the dashboard without blinking. A dead weight had formed inside my chest and though I didn't know it then, this weight would never leave me.

I had wanted only George. And because I knew he felt the same and because I could see a terrible window, I waited. And when George was grieving and had no room for me, I crushed everything inside of me that was huge and filled with joy into a tiny, dense point and I waited some more.

But George would not return to me. His eyes would look everywhere except at mine. I had lost him and so I left.

And I began to let him go. Hour by hour. Days into months. It was a physical sensation, like letting out the string of a kite. Except that the string was coming from my center.

He had parked the Honda behind the American Express building. It was there that George finally spoke all the words I had ever wanted him to say.

He said them all at once. "I love you. I am *in love* with you. You mean more to me than anything or anyone ever has and I am so sorry that I hurt you and pushed you away.

"I want to spend the rest of my life with you. Not hiding, not sneaking, and not waiting. I want everything and I want it only with you."

And because I had waited and waited and waited to hear him speak the words that I could *see* on his face and in his eyes; that his arms and neck and back and hands never withheld; and which was implicit in our relentless, insatiable, appetite for each other. Because of this, I turned to look at him.

And I saw that those words had always been inadequate; they were clichés.

They could not *begin* to name the trembling, almost orchestral longing, the magnitude, the need—all of it, utterly hopeless and complete.

I closed my eyes and wondered why I had ever made it about the words at all. Words like that were spoken every day; few people got to see what I saw right in front of me.

I opened my eyes and what I said was, *"Okay."*

And we didn't even stop by my apartment. We raced up the West Side Highway to his. We were traveling at the speed of an ambulance, as if this was the very definition of an emergency.

By the time we reached the end of the hallway and his door, we were desperate, clumsy, half-naked animals. Inside, we slammed the door shut with our bodies and dropped to the rug.

141

At midnight we showered. And we emerged from the steam a normal couple.

I noticed a new set of coffee mugs still on the counter, and when I went into the bedroom to throw on a T-shirt and shorts, I saw that the photograph of George with the boyfriend was gone. In the same frame was a photograph of me.

I had given it to him the year before and not seen it again until that moment.

Almost immediately, George introduced me to friends I'd never known he had. He displayed an easy, affectionate possessiveness; a hand on my shoulder, guiding; two hands suddenly around my waist, pulling me backward, reeling me in. The sex, rather, ceased. It was replaced with astonishing thoughtfulness.

What troubled me most was the way he now called me *honey*. As if this would be an acceptable term of endearment under even the most ideal circumstances. But we had come together as a couple beneath a mushroom cloud of infidelity, death, and now terminal disease.

Honey was the guy standing up in the metal rowboat, trying to keep his balance with his arms outstretched before him as he pleads with his wife and young daughter to join him out on the lake. Behind him, black clouds roil and grind; lightning flashes inside of them, thunder cracks the air. *C'mon guys, it'll be great, I promise!*

142

There was something *packaged* to us now. I simply could not believe a word of this new relationship. I didn't trust it. Whatever we had together, no matter how far from perfect it was, it had been forged from something real and it existed in a state between the wonderful and the terrible.

There had never been anything *ideal* about us except for the depth of our feelings and our instincts that we could believe in them. Now I was going through the motions of being one-half of an exceedingly happy couple. All the *words* I ever wanted to hear were there. I just didn't *see* them on his face anymore.

Sitting together in the parked car down in Battery Park City had been the proposal as well as the honeymoon.

And yet, there were benefits. We no longer had to confine the whole of our relationship to my living room sofa between the hours of noon and one in the afternoon. We did not have to choose between talking and feasting on that couch. And a handjob under the table at Mesa Grill would no longer have to suffice. I did not stand now at the window of my Battery Park City apartment and stare out at the World Trade towers and the

West Side Highway wondering what *he* was doing at that very moment. I would never again drink a bottle of vodka while listening to Julia Fordham's "Porcelain" over and over, her voice like a lighthouse in the inky blackness.

I had *exactly* what I asked for.

Oh, it may have taken an excruciating length of time and somebody may have died along the way. But didn't they always say nothing worth having comes easy?

I stood in the bathroom, which the dead boyfriend had designed, and I gazed at my own reflection in his mirror.

It was difficult to believe there hadn't been a physical change. A manifestation. I opened my mouth, stuck out my tongue and searched for signs that a cancer had come to take away the part of me that asks for things.

But I was only asking for a lighter sentence. I knew that the price for getting exactly what I asked for would be, eventually, losing it. I had won my lottery. But the tax would be unfathomably high.

Fall in Manhattan. Suddenly, smart woven coats in burnt umber, rust, ruddy brown, and a melancholy shade of green appear on the fashionable young ladies.

Athletic guys standing in line at the movie theater on Broadway and Eighteenth defiantly remain in shorts, refusing to grant the chill in the air the recognition it demands.

Brisk, blustery winds send fallen leaves, plastic coffee lids, and scraps of paper skittering along the sidewalks and then up into the air where they spiral at great heights.

This would be the first holiday season I had ever spent in New York as part of a couple. And for two or three weeks that October, I felt like perhaps the refreshing change of seasons had somehow had a clarifying effect on my mind. In no way did I believe things were suddenly right. But I had accepted George's illness in a way that I hadn't been sure I could.

Now his pills and frequent appointments with the doctor for blood work and minor alterations in his course of treatment all seemed nearly ordinary. As though he had a minor diabetes. Serious, but quite able to live a normal and vigorous life. George's stoic, *onward-Christian-soldiers* approach to his disease must have somehow demagnetized my banging iron pots of panic and terror. I was no longer waking up in the morning and being nearly knocked flat again by the horrible wave of reality.

Since the beginning of our new life, every day had begun with an overwhelming, crushing sense of doom.

"This can't be real," I would moan in the bathroom, from a place so low in my throat it seemed more a growl from my chest.

Then walking into the kitchen I was confronted with, *Oh yes it can!*

A new plastic pillbox, twenty-eight individual compartments.

The schedule imprinted on each lid—BREAKFAST, LUNCH, SNACK, DINNER—did not *normalize* the drugs; rather it had the opposite effect. It reminded me of what, exactly, I had given up to be with George. Never again can you have a normal *breakfast*—eggs, sunny-side up— when you have had *this* for breakfast. Once you are changed, so you remain.

But with the fall, so much of this sweltering negativity, this fever dream of relentless dread, seemed to be subsiding. Releasing me.

For the first time in months I went out for a walk, not an errand. Not to the doctor's office or to pick up prescriptions, I wasn't running around trying to find some insanely high-dose of vitamin C because Linus Pauling thought there might be something to it. I was just out.

I walked east along Thirteenth Street so that I would pass the Quad Cinema. I had always felt the Quad could show infomercials and ads for Korean and Lithuanian feminine hygiene products and I would stand in line to get inside, all because of their popcorn.

The Quad simply refused to allow that stick of butter to be pried from its fingers.

This was more comforting than one might think, in a time of tremendous insecurity. I had always gone to the Quad instead of to a therapist. Therapists, I felt, were like poodles: there were simply too many for them all to be good.

I walked down to Balducci's market to look at the tiny ears of corn, the exotic cheeses, and the pies. People were already shopping for Thanksgiving, still almost two weeks away. I saw an older gay man heft a pumpkin out of his cart at the checkout with the faintest look of satisfaction on his lips. He would be making a pie, I was certain of it, and no cans would be harmed in its creation.

I imagined him going into work the next morning with nutmeg still under his fingernails. He would casually run his thumb under his nose, pretending to scratch an itch. And there in the meeting he would get to inhale just a little bit more of his pie's soul.

I saw couples. Men together, women. I saw an old-fashioned *man and woman* walking with their arms linked, an English pram with a swaddled baby inside leading their way. I imagined they would be spending Thanksgiving with one set of parents. Whoever had the better set. After dinner it would only be four o'clock in the afternoon—too early to claim a mattress and curl up on top of it. Instead, everyone would sink into the sofa, drape themselves over the arms of overstuffed chairs like big cats—and there would be one or two of those, as well. The baby would be passed from chest to chest and each person would get a turn.

We would probably have Thanksgiving alone, but I could certainly think of worse things, having experienced many of them more than once. We could spend the night before in the kitchen making pies. Or just one pie. If I could actually lose myself in the act of *making a pie* with my boyfriend, I thought, I just might be able to do this.

To my surprise, Thanksgiving would not be just the two of us. It would be just the one of me.

George was going to his family's house in New Jersey. I had met George's two brothers but not his sister or his parents and it was obvious that George had not told them that he was no longer a grieving widower but a glowing newlywed. So to speak.

Actually, I didn't feel terrible about it. It wasn't like Thanksgiving with my boyfriend was being *taken away* from me. I'd never had Thanksgiving as an adult, so the loss was theoretical and abstract. It was a Monopoly-board loss.

What did make me feel terrible was the fuss he made before he left. George insisted on a festive Thanksgiving atmosphere in the apartment, even one cobbled together with deep orange candles and a tacky paper turkey on the glass dining table. He bought a pie. He pulled a roast chicken from its metallic-lined paper sack and pronounced, "Tah-dah! It's fresh roasted close enough."

That was the moment I felt most acutely that I was living a pretend life and not a true one.

George was putting on a little play so that I wouldn't be alone and depressed; just alone. It was like he was doing a magic trick, his right hand holding the cards out for me to choose, the left behind his back, fiddling with the trickery of a false deck. *Redirection,* is what they call it, and the only reason to do it is to fool a person into believing something they know can't be true.

When he left the next morning, I stood at the window overlooking Perry Street. As I watched him cross, it dawned on me that it was not *lonely* I felt, but *empty.*

I drank too much when I was alone. And the more I drank in general, the more often I just wanted to be alone. George had expected me to stay in the apartment while he was gone, but after less than an hour I felt I was performing on a stage and there was no audience. I was playing the role of the guy who is totally cool to be left alone on a holiday. So I walked home.

I had let go of my Battery Park City apartment and chosen a studio in the East Village. George had gone with me to look at it. It was unspoken yet understood that I would not give up my own apartment altogether, though I can't say I am sure why that was the case. And for this purpose, the apartment was perfect. It was a small, square box, less than three hundred square feet. A place to store clothes and take a nap.

As soon as I entered, something slid into place within me. In my hand was a bag containing a liter of vodka. I would drink Absolut and tonics with a splash of Rose's lime juice. That had been our drink, chosen by George on our very first date. He had also chosen our first song: "Manhattan Skyline," Julia Fordham.

I did put Julia Fordham on the stereo. I didn't see why I shouldn't.

My mistake was in underestimating the emotional force of a song you have already heard a thousand times. When I heard the song that night, I heard it with the ears I used to have. And I felt what I used to feel—that almost sickening blend of excitement and longing, mysteriously interwoven by not a little bit of bottom-of-the-stomach dread.

All came back to me: the powerful ache of needing to see him, be with him, even just on a street corner near his apartment that cost me eight dollars to reach by cab. And later, how hard I had tried to find the thing I could say that would unlock him from his grief and bring him back to me.

Over and over, I replayed the day of the boyfriend's wake. How back at the apartment George had been utterly leveled. Gone from his eyes was everything I had always seen in them, even when he sneezed. The apartment was filled with people—the boyfriend's mother, whom he hadn't seen for years. A brother. Others, strangers. Friends. And me. I sat on the sofa feeling fraudulent, like I did not belong.

Late in the day, George passed through the room and Madonna was singing "Cherish" on the stereo. And when she sang the words "Of always having you here in my life," George looked directly at me, mouthing the words, smiling a weary, heroic little smile, and winking.

That one exchange had been all I needed to fortify me through the year that lay ahead, a year in which George and I had sex only when I relentlessly groped beneath the covers after he had fallen asleep, when his body would respond before his mind could stop it.

His body, I knew, still did love me.

It was difficult to believe there had once been a time when I was not allowed to call him at the office because he would ejaculate in his slacks just hearing my voice.

George returned from his Thanksgiving and called me from the apartment in the afternoon. I let the machine pick up. He sounded playful and completely nonchalant but that was an act. George would have thought only one thing upon walking into that apartment and finding me gone: *Uh-oh.*

He would have thought about the period when I was gone entirely, just before he came to me with the Diagnosis. It had been, he told me, almost beyond his ability to endure.

George had been surprised by my ability to leave him. He had not seen that in me.

I waited until evening to call him and say I was busy with work and couldn't see him.

I worked as an advertising copywriter and though it was a consuming job, I was better at it than people knew. I had learned that my first idea was always my best; it was the one the clients bought, even if I came up with a dozen more later. Knowing this, I always trusted that first instinct. So I was able to do in an hour what another writer would agonize over for a week. In this way, I maintained a schedule that suited me. But I could always use it as an excuse. And I frequently did.

But I was back the next day as if I had never been gone, not even for a night. When I walked in the door he said, "Oh good, can you hand me the box from the top of the front closet?"

He was at the dining-room table writing checks. I had arrived at the perfect moment. I handed him the box and stuck my tongue out at the top of his head. And because his head did not then turn around with knowledge of what I had done, I felt a terrible regret and stood for a moment looking at his head, wishing I could take back the gesture, suddenly feeling only tender toward him, feeling he was precious and that any time spent away from him was an extravagant waste.

There we were: less than a week before Christmas.

New Yorkers are notoriously blasé about the holiday, though their very city is most famously dressed for the occasion. With every tree along Park Avenue not merely strung with lights but encased in them; strands of bulbs wrapped around and around and around each branch, every twig, right to the very tips. The unique anatomy of every tree, celebrated with light—the knotty elbow of a particular branch, a gleeful *V* that opens up with reaching fingers.

When I first moved to the city, the only Christmas present I ever needed was to hire a cab to drive me up and down the length of Park Avenue. With a bottle of cognac secreted in my coat pocket and the window all the way down, I pressed my face into the breeze like a dog. I closed my eyes for the longest moment, and when I opened them again I saw exactly what I had seen before. Block after block after block of *dazzling*. This was naked, full-frontal splendor.

Then there was the tree at Rockefeller Center. Dwarfed by the cluster of buildings that surround it, on the day the tree is lit, it instantly surpasses every one of them in magnitude. Almost more thrilling than the tree itself was the fact that so many people made a pilgrimage just to see it. A colorful winter sea of people, all of them exhaling elegant puffs of white smoke, like hopeful engines.

My love for Christmas had nothing to do with the birth of Jesus. It was the lights. It was the fact that grown people really did believe in Christmas miracles; longed for them even. New Yorkers, nonetheless.

So when George out of the blue pressed his body

tight up against my shoulder as we walked along Hudson Street, then reached down with both of his hands and found my one, taking my fingers between his own and squeezing my hand from all directions at once with precisely the force needed to say *Mine*, I was automatically euphoric. Ten fingers can overpower more than just one hand; ten fingers doing precisely the right thing, at the moment you least expect it, can make you forgive everything.

He had seen the tree stand up ahead and thought, *Why not get a tree tonight?* Disbelief was kicked right out by an eager, mindless, *yes, yes, yes* excitement. I wasn't going to ask why. The gift-horse law was instantly enacted.

We carried the tree home together. That was the word that he used, *home*. "Let's get this home, stick it up, and then watch a movie." Usually, he said, "the apartment" or "my apartment." Sometimes he even called it "Perry Street." He had never called it *our home* before. And while he hadn't said *our,* I'd heard it.

Halfway down the block he said, "Hold on," and let the peak of the tree drop to the sidewalk.

I continued holding the trunk. "Are you okay?"

He nodded, then leaned forward and placed his hands just above his knees, bent his legs. He took a deep breath, then another.

155

I held mine.

He straightened and smiled tightly at me. "It's nothing," he said. He didn't even say it. He mouthed the words, just like he had the day of the wake: *". . . of always having you here by my side."*

We continued walking toward the building but I was no longer aware of walking or carrying a tree. Suddenly, there was only a clock. It had appeared instantly, from nothing. And the red secondhand had begun to travel the dial in halting, unstoppable clicks.

And I knew: even if we are able to make us *really, really* good—there will be a limit.

There will be a day.

There will be an hour.

There will be a wake.

I thought George might lie down after we got upstairs but he didn't. Instead, we began extracting boxes from the cleverest storage spaces imaginable. A tree stand seemed to have been plucked from the space between two books. I could not imagine how he had devised such devious methods of hiding so great a volume of holiday paraphernalia.

"Steph did it," he said. "He loved what he called *finding space*."

I closed my eyes and let out a breath. That was *exactly* the feeling. I wanted to be *finding space*.

There was a magnificent optimism locked in the center of the phrase; the implication that there *was* space that did exist and could be found. The only question was, *How clever are you?* It was a phrase that nearly made me weep in relief. I steadied myself.

"Do you need this?" I asked, holding out a never-opened box of tinsel.

He was standing on a chair, level with the top of the tree and hanging the first strand of lights. He paused, arms outstretched, the string of bulbs bowing at the center. He looked hard at the box, wrinkled his forehead.

I smiled, seeing his eyes so busy in their search.

George had the most beautiful eyes. They were brown and therefore retained much of their information. You could not read them instantly like blue eyes. You had to keep looking, you had to *study*. Like searching for familiar forms in a darkened room. And there were sparks of mischief firing along the thin gold wires that streaked the iris. They were loyal eyes. Deeper, there was warmth, almost a glow. Just the crumbs from a fire, smoldering on. I loved most when his eyelashes twitched and he blinked, and suddenly *happiness* was there inside his eyes. Unmistakable. Like a single word printed on a clean white page. I used to love seeing that word in his eyes.

George finally recognized the box of tinsel I was holding. He said, "Oh no, I don't need that," and returned his attention to the tree.

We were going to spend Christmas alone together *at home*. We'd even talked about what to make for dinner.

"Should it be a roast beef?" I'd asked.

George had smiled at me, shrugged. "Could be, if that's what you'd like."

I said, "I just cannot wait to be the guy sitting in front of the fireplace with the Christmas tree over his shoulder and all the lights glittering away and the only present I have ever wanted is right here, where I can do with him exactly as I please." And I'd leaned over the single sofa cushion between us and moved for his neck.

He let me kiss his neck but it was a favor. I could sense him looking at the wall, waiting for me to finish.

I withdrew, but maintained my smile and said, "Yeah,

it'll be so amazing. I can't wait." And I slid back to my former position, slowly, as if my body had merely stretched briefly and returned.

"Augusten, listen," George began.

That was all he had to say for me to understand; there always was a new and terrible medical complication. A treatment-resilient *itis* or *oma* or *osis*.

So I was truly stunned when he said, "No, not that. It has nothing to do with my health."

I was blank.

How *sorry for me* his face became as the seconds emptied from the room, drained away from us forever.

But how could it have nothing to do with his health?

There *was* nothing besides his health.

The best and only *everything* that I had ever known depended solely and completely on the health of his every living cell.

When he told me what it was, I burst out laughing. It was from relief, more than anything else.

"Well, gee, Auggiedoggie, I never meant to upset you so much." He began to chuckle, tentatively at first, like a child at a fancy restaurant who watches the adults take a bite of food first, before venturing forward with his own fork.

Then he was laughing right along with me.

George and I would not be spending Christmas together after all. Actually, that had never been the plan. Because he always spent Christmas with his family.

My laughter trailed off and I asked, "But what about when you guys used to have Christmas?"

And George said, "He would never come. Sometimes he would move into a hotel room in case my family decided to stop over and see the apartment."

"You hid him away in a hotel room, like he was a dirty magazine you could stick under the mattress? *And he let you live?*"

"No, Augusten, it wasn't like that. My parents are great people but, you know, they don't need to know *everything* about me. They wouldn't be happy, and why upset them unnecessarily?"

I felt grateful, just then. Because I actually *hated* him at that moment and this hatred made me feel free. But the feeling was a vapor and it dispersed almost immediately.

I was facing the tree, which was reflected back into the room once again by the windows, now black with night.

The two candles on the dining-room table were lit, the flames so smooth they hardly quivered.

I didn't know what to say.

I just watched him, standing with his back to the tree

160

he had decorated. He had placed each ornament with such *exacting precision,* ever the investment banker.

No, that's not it, I thought.

He had placed each ornament with *excruciating care.* Because it was the one and the only thing he could make perfect.

He would turn his back on this tree and leave this home—leave me, *leave us*; this family he built himself. He would leave us behind on Christmas Day so that he could be by himself with the family that he came with.

It was Christmas Eve and he was leaving for his parents' house. We stood beside the front door. He was in his black wool coat, the one he wore over his suits to the office. His face was strained and he looked so tired. I could see that he felt both powerless and guilty.

I faced him and took one lapel in each fist, raised them up tall. I adjusted his scarf at the nape, making sure it covered any naked skin.

His black leather gloves were already on his hands, which were hanging straight down at his sides. His overall stiffness was endearing, childlike.

He had known about Christmas all along but had not been able to tell me because I was so excited.

He chose what had seemed to him to be the most humane course of action. He allowed me to have my perfect New York City Christmas for as long as he possibly could.

And I had our first Christmas so fully imagined that it had begun to feel more like a memory than a fantasy.

I knew how the table would be set and I could even see how the slices of roast beef would fold onto the plates.

I knew that he would have a second piece of pie.

And that we would then sit on the floor in front of the fire.

His glittering, beautiful tree would stand in the corner and throw its light and sparkle all over our backs.

And as I looked at his face lit by the fire, I would start to feel myself falling backward into the person I used to be, before I was disfigured by my own appalling dread.

George would glance at me and he would freeze. I would see the wires in his eyes begin to glow as he realized that I was suddenly, finally, truly right there beside him. And not still a few steps ahead, in the inevitable future.

He would begin to tremble very slightly.

And my eyes would travel to his neck, and down the length of it.

His whole body would shudder.

And he would close his eyes and feel my hands on him, long before they ever reached his skin.

Much later, we would have a snack. We would eat it wordlessly, standing side-by-side in the wedge of light that you are given when the refrigerator door is opened in the middle of the night.

As we stood by the front door, I carefully adjusted a lock of George's hair and looked into his eyes and without saying one word—by only feeling it, by truly meaning it—I thanked him for giving me exactly the Christmas I had dreamed of.

Because day after day as I imagined it, I always forgot one little detail: our virus.

In my mind, on our first Christmas as a family, it was always just the *two* of us.

And as far as my eyes could see in any direction, there was only more, and more, and more.

Slowly, I leaned toward him, then against, then into.

"Merry Christmas," I said, my voice soft, deep; *vertical, not horizontal.*

My mouth was pressed against his ear. I felt the tiny hairs on his earlobe scratch at my lips.

My chest was pressed against his; my heart directly over his.

And then. I lifted my arms off of him entirely, withdrew my hands from his shoulders.

I pulled away from him, slow, slow, to see his face.

And he was standing perfectly still in his long black coat.

But his head was back, neck arched.

And his eyes were closed.

And his mouth was open so that he could breathe.

And I could see so clearly that he was in both ecstasy and astonishment at once.

His eyelashes twitched.

And he blinked.

And suddenly *happiness* was inside his eyes.

Unmistakable.

Like a single word printed on a clean white page.

And because there was so much to say that would never be said; because his eyes flashed with tears and because he knew that I was suddenly, finally and truly right there beside him, his voice cracked as he spoke.

"I was hoping it was you."

I never chose a life with George. *There had never been a choice to make.*

He had been there all along, woven into the fabric of my future.

Destiny.

I would have laughed in your face.

I did not leave cookies out for Santa Claus.

And I did not believe in destiny.

But.

When Santa is suddenly standing right in front of you, soot from *your* chimney staining his fine red suit and he is flushed and breathing hard and smells like frost and sweat and smoke and his jacket is linted with coarse reindeer hairs and there is reindeer shit on his boots and his eyes twinkle with preposterous joy, you simply cannot say, *"I don't believe in you,"* and turn your back on him.

    Because he will grip you by the shoulders and wrench you around and he will bring his bristly mouth to yours and blow
stars
      down your throat
            until
               you are so full
                   of
                     light.

Silent Night

*P*OSSIBLY BECAUSE I hadn't had a drink in ten years, I no longer peed in the kitchen sink, blew my nose on my T-shirt, or wet the bed. I was now fully domesticated with a family that included one Dennis, two French bulldogs, a station wagon, and a septic tank. I'd even had my first colonoscopy. It just doesn't get more grown-up than that.

So, was it possible that I hadn't done *anything* for Christmas since *just before George died?*

That was ten years ago.

One decade.

This was not "a healing interim"; it was pathologically morbid.

It was perhaps time for some jolly.

Dennis and I had spent two years building our home in western Massachusetts—plaster walls, beadboard ceilings, and paint imported from Holland. Even the inside of each closet had layers of crown molding that had been cut by hand. As my brother so aptly put it, "It's a house suitable for queers."

My older brother and I built our houses at the same time on the same street, just two doors apart. Ours was the gay house, with oiled soapstone counters and a wildflower garden lit by a copper gas lantern barely bright enough to help you see the keyhole on the door; his was a hetero cement-clad monolith with an active steam pipe over the front door and xenon vapor gas discharge exterior floodlights that illuminated his wooded backyard like an Ikea parking lot.

With each imported-from-Cincinnati brass push-button light switch plate we installed, I felt six Phillips-head screw revolutions farther away from every bad thing that had ever happened to me. Tentatively, I began pretending I was entering the "After" stage of my life—the part with brocade window treatments and shiny German faucets. Where the worst thing that could happen was getting into a *discussion* with another shopper at Whole Foods over the last container of edamame.

Even my taste in furniture buffered me from

catastrophe—I liked old things. Chairs and tables with nicks and stains and dents. I liked seeing where the split leg of the dresser had been so carefully glued back together. And I loved the table beside the sofa; if you put a glass of water on it, the glass would gradually slide onto the floor. Otherwise, you didn't really see that it was lopsided. I figured, if this crap can survive all those other families for so many years, surely it can survive one of me for just this life.

A major benefit of building a house with Dennis is that he made a lot of the choices, and they were very fine choices. In fact, everything I loved about the house had been his idea. It occurred to me that if some Suburban-careening dot-com bitch chatting away on her cell phone happened to plow into him on the Merritt Parkway, sending our little Audi somersaulting into Vermont, I would find a certain measure of comfort in this house, which contained so much of him. This ran counter to my experience with George, whose mother had cleaned and emptied the apartment within hours of his body reaching room temperature.

Dennis and I had been together for six years. And nothing horrible had happened. It was the longest I had ever gone in my life without needing an emergency room, a law enforcement official, or a funeral home. A Christmas tree would be the bow on the package. More than anything else, it was a symbolic way of saying, *"Disaster? I am no longer your bitch."*

The more I thought about it the more I felt I was almost *owed* a real and proper Christmas.

Dennis, however, was less than enthusiastic about the whole idea. A tree would shed needles and make a mess. Besides, we didn't own any ornaments or lights, not even a tree stand. "And a fresh tree is going to need watering. Are you going to be the one making sure it has fresh water every day?"

"It's not a pet, it's just a dead tree," I cried.

But there was something else. His name was Jesus.

Dennis was an atheist. He didn't believed in God, so the idea of celebrating the birth of the Son of God, Jesus Christ, our Lord and Savior felt entirely absurd, like throwing a *bar mitzvah* for the Easter Bunny.

Now, I was about as far from being *Christian* as a person could be while still living outside the walls of a supermax prison. I didn't believe in God, either. But wasn't that all the more reason to saw down a living tree and truss it with environmentally unfriendly lights? Shit, we could even make it an olive tree.

"Look," I said, "I just want a little tree. With some pretty lights. And a few sparkly balls. We don't even have to have a star on top if that's too Jesus of Nazareth for you."

He knew I could talk him into almost anything. "I don't want to celebrate the big Christian holiday," he mumbled, frowning.

"I'm not suggesting we set up a nativity scene on the mantel and then go bomb an abortion clinic. I just want a little tree. That's all."

And when he smiled just a little, I added, "Come on, it will be fun."

The smile was still there but his eyes flashed with caution.

I had used that exact phrase—*it will be fun*—about going boating on the Connecticut River with my brother early in the summer. Dennis had never learned to swim and hated the water, but he figured it would be okay "for an hour or so," and reluctantly agreed.

The grim, fatiguing seven-hour boat ride was not merely a *memory* for him, but a ropy psychic scar.

Finally, I just told him, "I have always loved Christmas. Even when I was in my twenties and trying to be very cool and anti-Christmas, secretly, I still loved it. And I know that's kind of idiotic, but there you go. I mean, I buy all of it: the cheesy music, the gaudy lights, and the spray snow, especially the spray snow. So the thing is, I have loved Christmas my entire life, and yet? Every single one has really been kind of hideous. Or maybe *hideous* isn't the word. Maybe it's more like,

171

cataclysmic. It's like I have a genuine Christmas *curse* or something. All I want is just one good, normal, happy holiday. A little one."

His eyes had softened and he walked over to the counter and grabbed the car keys. "Ready to go get our first Christmas tree?"

The smell of fresh balsam was overwhelming as we stepped out of the car. Atkins Market, a former roadside apple stand that got ambitious and now peddled lobster tails and clever mustard, had a parking lot full of fresh-cut trees.

Ropes of soft white bulbs lit the area and the ground was thick with needles and sawed-off lower branches. It was this makeshift cocoon of bare-bulb lighting along with the tree carnage and balsam-stained air that made me realize, this was like the animal-friendly equivalent of a whaling vessel.

Standing beneath that halo of light, I suddenly felt *observed.* I imagined Greenpeace activists hiding in the darkness of the surrounding orchard, waiting to pummel us with sticks and frozen Granny Smith apples.

I woke up on my right side, facing away from the wall of windows. I thought: *It's bright. I've overslept.* And I had, it was nearly eight thirty. The dogs were nestled deep into the down comforter. Bentley, who was normally awake at first light, excited about his morning walk, merely glanced at me as I climbed from the bed and walked to the next room.

Dennis was sitting at his desk. He was working and appeared to have been awake for hours. "Oh, hi there," he said. "I didn't hear you wake up."

"Just now. Did you not sleep? Why are you already up?"

He nodded at the stack of papers, envelopes, and bills on his desk. "The Amex bill. Some accounting things for Ira that I was supposed to send him last week, just a lot of paperwork."

Because the word *accounting* makes me want to shoot heroin, I nodded blankly and smiled, turned right, and began down the stairs to my own office.

Halfway down, I became aware of the difference in temperature; it had been comfortable upstairs but already it was *chilly* down there.

Winter in New England, I thought. *Heat rises.*

And then I saw the dazzling display of lights. Dennis had been the last one to bed; I hadn't known he'd kept the tree lit.

The blinking lights were reflected across the glossy finish of our dark wood floors. Red, green, blue, yellow, purple—the colors seemed to be spreading from the shadows beneath the sofa, magically swirling, glistening and glittering throughout the main downstairs living area.

Kitchen, dining room, living room—all one space— shimmered with this wondrous Christmas ether. Even the wet-gloss baseboards and walls were splattered with twinkling lights.

I was momentarily stunned, locked in place at the bottom of the stairs, my right hand still on the banister, my body turned in witness. There was so much blinking, sliding, sparkling color; jewels flowing into jewels, the room awash in luminosity, hazy rings of glow floating everywhere.

It was beautiful in a way that made me hold my breath; the body's response was to choose *seeing* over breathing. My eyes understood that what I was seeing was rare, significant.

Yet somehow, also, incorrect.

Like looking up at the night sky and seeing, there beside the moon, a nebula of silvery, blue lights; a nursery of baby stars where there had always been only shadow.

It was magnificent.

Then I understood, and it was appalling.

The lights *were* bleeding out from beneath the sofa and the table and all the legs of every chair. They were liquefied. The shadows had melted, their dark tails dissolved into a rippling, expanding lake of saturated color.

The floor, impossibly, was beneath *inches* of shimmering water.

Our new house, the home we had built together over two years and just finished, was flooded.

I watched waves glide beneath the dining table and soak into the carpet, ocean into sand. I remained motionless at the bottom of the stairs in a kind of paralysis of disbelief.

Two of the things Dennis hated most in the world— water and Christmas—had joined forces to ruin his new home.

I had always had the oddest feeling—consider it knowledge—that if I were ever to find myself inside the cockpit of a 767 with two dead pilots and a few hundred passengers in the cabin behind me, I would absolutely be able to land the ninety-thousand-pound jet.

And I would do it without deploying those ridiculous yellow rubber chutes.

I could see the landing in my mind: the sickening seesaw of the wings as I made my approach in a heavy crosswind, the thought-pulverizing spced of the geography's approach and then at the last possible moment, the bending of probability itself, the crack of logic's irrefutable spine, and the instantaneous elimination of all potential outcomes except for one: mine. The moment crowned and I delivered it—the perfect, elegant lift of the magnificent nose *just so.*

Almost *arrogant.*

The settling of the wings, instantaneous and in unison; like twin sisters suddenly deciding to behave perfectly and in flawless cooperation.

The coiled spring every passenger felt at their very center, held in place by the weight of breath, before the rear tires hit the tarmac, bouncing once.

The wheels slamming down once more, this time with permanence; *they will not bounce again.* The nose gently settling and the plane screaming defiantly down the runway, a gleaming triumph of flashing sun streaks.

Failure, destruction, ruination—the statistically probable outcome—was a mere vapor trail, mist consumed by the roiling air left in the plane's wake.

I would land that 767.

But frozen at the bottom of the stairs in my own home, transfixed by the ruin, I couldn't do a thing.

I snapped the hell out of it.

My hand left the smooth, polished curve of the banister's volute at the bottom of the stairs and I ran past the old hutch where we kept cookbooks and plates. It had an ancient mouse hole on the side. You certainly couldn't call it *fancy*. But many people before me had owned it and kept it safe. And it was standing in water.

As I ran, my feet kicked up dual arches of water so tall they nearly touched the ceiling. It was as though I was running through the surf. It was automatically joyous, and then horrifying.

I reached the kitchen sink. Water was escaping from beneath the under-sink cabinet doors. More water than could ever flow out the faucet. A sheet of water; it cascaded. How could there possibly be so much of it?

I experienced a moment of *doubt*.

It was like an infection, a germ received in an

179

unwanted touch. *This is too much for me.* I spoke the words in my mind.

And because I did, suddenly it was.

I called for Dennis. "You have to get down here right now, hurry. It's an emergency. But leave the dogs upstairs, lock them in the bedroom."

Alarm in his voice: "What did you say?"

My eyes fixed on the torrent of water spilling over the kitchen floor. The floor itself was now warped: the center of each wide floorboard swollen into a peak, then cupped into a valley. I shouted, "Lock the dogs in the bedroom and come down here. Hurry. Right now, do it."

I was barking orders like a fireman. But my sense had left me and so had my courage.

The plane was beginning to lose altitude, the nose dipping.

I backed out of the kitchen and turned around. Dennis was at the bottom of the stairs, heaving, unable to catch his breath, as his eyes surveyed the room.

He stood where I had stood, he absorbed what I could not.

He ran to the head of the table, stopped.

He could go no farther.

He brought both of his hands to his mouth, his fingers touching the bottom lip.

"No, no, no, no, no, no, no, no, no, no, no, no, no,"

his voice warbled, and what began as a whisper was almost instantly a howl; a sound that resonated with loss and terrible ache. And then it broke and he gasped for air and the wail came back, "Aw, no, why? Why? Why-hy-hy?" There was no mistaking the shock, horror, disbelief, pain, agony, failure—the abrupt removal of what we had formed with our own hands: home.

His knees buckled and I watched as he collapsed, doubled over as though shot in the stomach. But he raised his head so that he could see—he could not look away.

His hands now covered his face but his eyes were wide open, peering through the spaces between his fingers. He was trembling.

He screamed and he wailed and he moaned and he wept.

Nobody had died. It was only a house. We were not injured. The dogs were okay. Yet none of that seemed to matter. It *should* have mattered. All of those facts ought to have figured into the final accounting. But the math was immediate and the sum was irreversible.

Worse things had happened to me. But this was the worst moment of my life—seeing him like this was exactly the most I could take. Not one more thing could happen or I would break.

I had no idea what to do next.

Layered over this awareness, overlapping this recognition was a wave, a sensation that something was gathering. There was an alignment, a condensation, and it expanded until it was the only thing: the pilot had regained consciousness.

The pilot lunged toward the center panel, his right hand gripping the throttle, sliding it forward. The sound of the engines filled the world.

He pulled back on the wheel, which lifted the nose abruptly. The steel springs deep inside the cushion dug into his back.

I gripped Dennis by his arms and pulled him to a standing position.

He seemed unaware of me, his hands again covering his mouth, his eyes, wide and horrified and unblinking, fixed on the water at his feet, water in the act of destruction, water slaying us.

I wedged my body between him and what he was seeing; I gripped his wrists, pulled his hands from his face and replaced them with my own hands, one on each cheek. I angled his head so he had to look at me.

He blinked, and suddenly he was there.

I spoke in a low, firm voice. "Come with me. Do *exactly* what I say."

He nodded.

I nudged him forward, through the deep water and

then up the stairs. I clung to him, lightly pushing, like a border collie.

The thick wool carpeting on the treads was an instant relief, which was when I realized my bare feet were so cold they were numb.

When we reached the landing, I opened the bedroom door and steered him through. I directed him to the bed, angled him around so that the mattress was against the backs of his knees, then I pushed him down to a seated position. He stared blankly ahead. Like he was broken and didn't work anymore. But I could not think about that.

I climbed onto the bed and pulled him up after me. His body was rigid with resistance. I shoved him flat. Then I turned onto my right side, pressed up hard against him and whispered in his ear. "Listen to me. It's going to be okay. We will rebuild. We will rebuild the house. And we will make it better than it is. This is okay. It's just a house. It's just stuff. It's only wood. I promise you, we're going to be okay. Have I ever been wrong? Even once?"

I was betting that in his current state, he wouldn't think too long about this one.

And I could feel the shock settle. I could physically *feel* that terrible, mindless fear and palsy of the soul depart. It was as if I had given him an injection, a sedative.

He took a deep breath and when he let it out, I recognized his eyes again.

And then I knew we were past that awful place, the Fear Capsule, and would not return.

I waited another long moment. And then I said, "Okay, get the fuck up *now,* we have to turn that water off."

Originally, we were just going to let the basement be a basement. But then: *There are French doors that open onto the backyard—let's build a stone patio! And we could put a bathroom next to the hot water heater, and a media room—get a large flat-screen for the wall, surround sound.*

So we'd finished half the basement and left the rest for storage.

Dennis had the stairway leading down lined with beadboard, which spread onto one wall and covered the entire ceiling. It took the contractor months because every line had to flow perfectly into every other. There was a wall of bookcases, made by hand, with roomy cabinets below.

We'd installed the speakers for the surround sound, but not yet the television.

It was also the only room in the house with wall-to-wall carpeting; a thick New Zealand wool in a spectacularly cool green and red plaid. I had been terrified of plaid wall-to-wall carpeting. "It won't look like a rec room," he had promised.

But as I walked down the soggy stairway into the basement, I heard disturbing sounds—fluids in motion, weaponized water. Once I reached the bottom I saw that it was, in fact, raining.

Water was dripping through all the spaces between the beadboard, every joint, each section where one piece of hand-planed wood met another. So much water was raining down that is was officially a storm. I couldn't see all the way to the other side of the room.

The thick wool carpet had not absorbed the water— it was beneath it like some kind of bog moss.

Whole sheets of paint had welted and were peeling away from the plaster walls, hanging limply. It was like a third-degree burn. The plaster itself was curdling, dissolving. There was so much water, the windows and French doors overlooking the backyard were coated with condensation.

Yet I noted these details with only remote interest and complete detachment. The part of me that would have made a superb serial killer was now activated. I walked straight ahead, right through the rain. I felt no sadness. I felt nothing.

I was the pilot peeling the copilot's violently severed

face off the instrument panel, slinging it into the corner like a wet leather rag, then nonchalantly wiping the blood from the altimeter.

I located the valve in the far corner of the basement and twisted the knob counterclockwise as far as it would go. This provided me with an unexpected jolt—was it *revenge*? No, not revenge, not nearly. But I had clenched my teeth all the same and felt that primal *biting-into-a-steak* satisfaction.

It was control.

The valve restored my sense that all was right in the universe; turning it stopped sanity, order, and familiarity from draining out of my life altogether.

I jogged back through the sloshy Tollund Man basement and up the mushy steps onto the main floor. Dennis was feebly struggling with the mop—nothing more than a lengthy sponge on a stick. There was a flatness to his face, like it had been sculpted from clay and only half finished, abandoned before the finer details were added. He clearly hadn't realized that we were long past the *sponge mop* stage. We were now at *drainage,* and we could well reach *wrecking ball* by nightfall.

I lunged toward him. "Fuck the mop," I said, snatching it from his hands and tossing it on the floor, behind me. "We have to get this water out of here and we have to get it out *now.*"

It was as if I had a plan, knew what I was doing. Mine was the voice of Command, the voice of Action. I listened to it myself, curious and obedient, having no idea what it would say next.

I dropped to the floor at the base of the Christmas tree in front of the French doors leading out to the deck. I yanked hard on the green cord for the lights, jerking it from the wall outlet. Then I wrapped my arms around the trunk of the tree and carefully slid it away from the doors. Dennis asked, "What are you doing with that?"

"Open the doors," I told him.

The deck was covered with deep snow and it was freezing outside. He couldn't understand why I wanted the doors open so he was stuck, immobile.

I leaped up and unlocked the doors myself, then pried them open. I was immune to the blast of icy morning air. All that mattered was: now, we had an exit for the water.

I needed something large and flat. Like a dustpan. *Exactly* like one, in fact. So I ran down the mudroom hallway to the garage, plucked the dustpan from its hanger on the wall and returned to the kitchen. I squatted and began to shovel water onto the deck. It worked, but it did not work well enough. Better than the twenty rolls of paper towels we'd thrown down whole, but not good enough.

I dropped the dustpan and grabbed the phone to call my brother. Dennis picked up the dustpan and continued to flap water out to the deck. When my brother answered I yelled into the phone, "The house flooded. Get up here with stuff."

My brother replied, "Okay, I'll be right there."

I hung up.

My brother was exactly the brother you wanted to have in the event of a flat tire or the complete collapse of society. Whether you needed automatic weapons, advanced knowledge of nuclear systems, or just an industrial sump pump, he was the one to call. His Asperger's syndrome endowed him with certain mechanical qualities—a detached monotone, either no empathy or no way to express it, an obsessive, software-loop kind of pursuit of ever-changing interests. He also shared a special kinship with all things engineered.

While he'd never seen *Friends* and would probably tear pages from *Anna Karenina* to wipe oil off a dipstick, ask him about that "Length Fractionation of Carbon Nanotubes Using Centrifugation" article in *Advanced Materials* magazine and he'd never shut up.

Though we lived only two houses apart, it would take him a good fifteen minutes. He would have equipment to locate and transport. Possibly, he would have to zip into an encapsulating chemical or biohazard suit.

Watching Dennis continue to dustpan water out of the house, I worried we may have already entered the wrecking ball stage. All this water had been sitting on the floors for hours—who knew how many?

I couldn't wait even fifteen minutes for my brother. I was going to have to do something I never, not even in my most terrifying nightmares, imagined: I was going to have to ask one of our neighbors for help. Carleen.

She was a professor. At the very least, she would be able to think of a better tool than a dustpan to get rid of the water.

I stumbled out of the garage wearing clumsy winter boots and no socks. My feet were sliding around inside them and I kept tripping. It felt like weeks had passed since I'd been outside, which is how I must have looked: pale, unshaven, wild-eyed, out of breath.

I was lumbering down my driveway when I saw Carleen sitting on the steps of her front porch, despite the cold. She was wearing a thick bathrobe and held a mug of coffee in her hand.

She resembled everything I had tried to create that was now destroyed.

As I walked, then jogged, across our yard to hers, I thought, *I made Dennis leave New York City and build a house with me in Massachusetts. And then I destroyed it all because that is what I do—attract disaster.*

As I neared Carleen, I could no longer see her. I could see only Dennis, doubled over on the floor and sobbing, "No, no, no." Some part of him would be warped now, like the floors. The part that believed in me and thought we could build a life. The part that made it unscathed through forty-four years.

Then I was standing in front of Carleen, ragged and panting. My past had hunted me down and it had found me.

It turned out, in my new *There's meatloaf in the freezer!* life, the meatloaf was actually just a dead cat wrapped in aluminum foil.

The furniture that had outlasted three centuries was right now splitting apart in my living room as it soaked up my water. Soon, it all would crash through the floor into the basement, with Dennis on top, impaled by my colonial fireplace poker.

What did I say to Carleen? I don't remember. All that remains is this: she rose from the steps and moved to her front door, all at once. She was a blur, in motion. She held the coffee out, away from her. And her robe was airborne around the edges.

With her hand on the doorknob, she turned and looked over her left shoulder and said, "We'll be right there."

The way she said it, or maybe the way she moved—almost choreographed, as though all her life she had known that this moment was coming—made me certain she would know what to do with all of our terrible water.

As I headed back inside, I wondered how the day would ever end. I hadn't had that feeling for years. Not since I'd stopped drinking.

I remembered, no matter how impossible it seemed that any given day would end, it always did. This one would, too.

Even worse, now I knew things could happen in the night. Harm could reach you no matter how insulated you thought you were. It could change you. It could *take*.

When Carleen arrived a few moments later, she brought her transplanted California surfer-dude blond husband, Henry, and her Shop-Vac. Henry was holding what appeared to be every bath towel they owned, each perfectly folded.

I saw the slightest widening of her eyes as she surveyed the damage, but she said nothing. I had learned this about Carleen: if it was a rainy day, she would never say, *"It sure is a rainy day."*

She simply began to assemble the vacuum and then she plugged it in. Carleen was like a trauma surgeon: *"Yeah, it's really never a good idea to French kiss any dog you don't know, but especially not a Presa Canario. Well, let's see if we can't get a temporary face sewn in place for you."*

She raked the vacuum across the floor in wide, even strokes, sweeping the room in a logical grid. And when I saw this I thought, thank God we live next door to somebody with a Ph.D. I had lived in Manhattan for nearly ten years before I even *realized* it was laid out in a grid. Then Dennis had to explain its advantage.

In ten minutes, all the standing water was gone. It had been simple. She didn't need a sponge mop or a dustpan or twenty rolls of paper towels.

I'd managed to close the French doors and turn the heat all the way up.

But that is fairly all I did.

Perhaps I oversold myself a little as a pilot. Maybe I was the airsick passenger in the back of the plane, the one who has lifted all the barf bags from the surrounding seats and is filling them up one by one.

It wasn't only that Carleen owned a Shop-Vac. I could have owned a Shop-Vac. The difference was, she cleaned up all the water with it.

While I most certainly would have electrocuted us all.

My brother descended a few moments after the last of the water had been sucked away. He was driving a British military Land Rover that was hauling a trailer behind it. Instead of parking on the driveway, he plowed straight across it and onto the side yard, then down and around into the back. The wide, toothy tires devoured chunks of half-frozen yard, mixing them in with snow.

He entered the house like a weather system, a supercell thunderstorm complete with rotating cloud bands and downbursts. At six-three and well over two-hundred pounds, his long legs and huge feet enabled him to travel to the center of the space in two or three great, lumbering strides.

He stood perfectly straight, looming over every-thing, his eyes not even blinking behind the thick lenses of his glasses. He was expression-neutral and made no sound as he surveyed the room, instantly collecting vast amounts of data, like a barcode scanner at a supermar-ket checkout.

Some sort of globally convergent infeasible-interior-point predictor-corrector algorithm must have switched in his mind, because all at once, he zeroed in on our Christmas tree.

With great purpose, he moved to the French doors. They seemed to explode open at his touch.

Just then, he noticed Henry and Carleen standing in the kitchen. "Oh, huh," he said. "Well, hi, I guess."

Carleen smiled at him, and though he was unable to tell, it was a fully genuine, cannot-be-helped kind of smile. "Hi, John."

She had always liked my brother. "He's direct, that's what I love about him. You always know exactly where you stand with John."

"Yeah, it's quite the mess in here. What happened? Did a pipe burst?" he asked.

"We don't know yet. It came from under the sink but the plumbing in the rest of the house still works, so who the fuck knows."

"You think maybe your fancy queer faucet turned

against you?" He nodded his head at our kitchen sink, the gleaming nickel Franke faucet.

"It wasn't that," I said, annoyed. It was too lovely to cause trouble; it wasn't some garbage-faucet from Wal-Mart. But now that I glanced over at it again, there seemed to be something smug in its gleam.

He shrugged. "Huh. Well, in any case, we have to get everything out of here."

And as suddenly as the words had left his mouth, his gargantuan paw gripped the neck of the Christmas tree. He hoisted it straight up, high into the air. The tree stand slid off and crashed to the floor as my brother maneuvered the tree over his shoulder, some-what like a javelin and hurled it onto the deck and into the snow that was packed into a drift against the railing.

Christmas balls popped free of their hangers and flew in all directions. Some rolled back into the house, others sunk into the snow on the deck. Most, though, slipped through the railing and shattered against the stone pa-tio below.

A snarl of lights trailed from the branches, the tiny bulbs crushed into colorful dust beneath his boots.

Strands of silver tinsel blew from the tree and lifted into the air above the backyard. As they were carried higher and still higher, these strands looked not like tinsel anymore, but rather like scratches; tears in the very fabric of everything.

It was an effort for Dennis to even speak, he was so dumbfounded. "What did you do *that* for?"

My brother turned and looked out at the tree. We all did. There was something quite shocking, even disturbing about it.

It was almost as if my grandmother had come to spend Christmas with us, dressed in her very best outfit and wearing her favorite jewelry—her charm bracelet, her gold and jade rings—and we'd gone and beaten the hell out of her then tossed her broken body into a snowbank. There was just something plain old *awful* about it.

I hadn't felt this way as a child when my mother hurled the Christmas tree off the deck; then it had seemed thrilling. *Maybe she'll burn down the house!*

My brother grunted and said, "Well, you really oughtta have a fake tree like we do. They're much less trouble, they don't mess up the house, and they're better for the environment."

I stared at him, picturing a Chinese Christmas tree factory located on a former lake bed or wildlife preserve, spewing toxic green smoke into the unregulated air; the freshly stamped trees being hoisted by forklift onto tractor trailers so they could be driven four hundred miles to the port where they would be loaded onto an oil-leaking ship and taken to America.

Yeah, I was *sure* they were better for the environment.

He strode around the dining room table, reached over, and hoisted the huge, overstuffed slip-covered lounge chair right off the floor and into the air, holding it steady beside his large hairy head. He barked, "C'mon, what the fuck are you all just standing there for? Don't you understand? We have to get every single item up off the floor and out of this room. Mush, mush," he shouted. "Each one of you, grab something and take it into the garage or throw it onto the deck with the tree."

We did.

And we fell into a silent rhythm, from living room to garage; chair, table, chest. As we worked, a television commercial was irritatingly playing on a loop in my head.

This used to happen to me as a child. Without trying or even wanting to, I automatically memorized every word of every commercial. The difference was, back then I was compelled to act them out.

"Water can be more damaging than fire. When you have a flood or serious water damage, Call ServePro. When fire and water take control of your life, we help you take it back. Serve-Pro. Like it never even happened."

It was that last line that I kept repeating. *"ServePro. Like it never even happened."*

Only after ten or fifteen minutes of this refrain rat-on-a-treadmilling through my brain did I say, "Wait a minute," and run from the room, into my office.

I was stunned that the Internet still worked. Somehow, I had assumed the flood had taken everything away, even Google.

When I returned, I smiled at Dennis. "The Cavalry is coming," I told him. "They'll be here in two hours."

With the room now stunningly empty and all our furniture stacked and piled in the garage, only the heavy, soaked rugs remained. My brother squatted down and began to roll, and then bunch the first rug up into a transportable mound. "I'll take all the rugs down to my house and lay them out on the radiant heat flooring in the basement where they can dry."

And all our rugs traveled by British military Land Rover past one mailbox, then another, and down my brother's long driveway and straight into one of his four garages.

Dennis appeared to be in shock so I said, "He may be something of a bull in a china shop but when your china shop is being held up at gunpoint by thugs, you'll be awfully glad you have a thousand-pound bull behind the counter, snorting and furious and ready to stampede."

Dennis nodded because it was true.

Carleen and Henry slipped out to take care of their two kids. And the man who literally built our house stopped by. I'd called him because I had developed a psychological dependence on him and it seemed to me he could fix everything. But he could do little more than stand in morbid awe and be appalled.

This would be our lump of coal and reindeer-hit-by-car sandwiches Christmas. Just exactly like all the motherfucking rest of them.

ServePro arrived in a large Ghostbusters' van. They wore uniforms and carried precision instruments with long, sharp probes that could be inserted into wood, to test its moisture content. After entering the house, they signaled one another using hand gestures and then dispersed; a couple went into the rear, two more downstairs to the basement. The sergeant stayed with me and I found his presence comforting. His unchanging facial expression—one of serious concentration but no surprise—made me feel that perhaps our water damage was less severe than I thought. Maybe he would tell us to lay newspapers on the floor over night to soak up any remaining moisture. Maybe he would say, *"Pay no mind to the deformity of floorboards; they'll spring back into shape in a couple of days."*

Instead, he reached for his walkie-talkie and recalled the rest of the troop.

That's when they brought out the hatchets.

Whole chunks of ceiling were removed, baseboards pried away from walls. Dennis's prized carpet was ripped from the floor like a scab and carpet nails shot like sparks around the room.

When they finally left, the house had been filleted, nine industrial dehumidifiers and high-output drying fans had been left behind and the heat had been turned up to ninety.

It was now evening and the day was not destroyed, it was merely over. The house would live.

In bed that night, the walls and windows vibrated, as did the bed itself. This was because the dehumidification equipment, which would need to run twenty-four hours a day for a minimum of two weeks, sounded and felt like a jet engine was loose in the house. Upstairs with the bedroom door closed, we were somewhat isolated from the sound, but there would be no escaping the deep, endless vibrations I could feel in my liver.

Dennis lay flat on his back with his arms straight out from his sides. The dogs stood on his chest and licked his head. He was still wet from the shower, so they were able to get a drink, too.

"You know who you look like right now, especially in your boxers?"

He said, "Who?" then, "Blech, not my teeth, Cow."

I smirked and said, "Jesus. With your arms straight out like that."

"Very funny, ha ha," he said.

Then I asked him, "Do you think I could become a Christian or is it too late for me?"

"Why do you want to become a Christian?"

"Because what Carleen did for us was very Christian."

"You're not Carleen."

I was not Carleen.

After caring for her children, Carleen had returned. She was polished and well dressed and I saw at once how such a person no longer belonged in our house. It was a house for dirty guys in overalls once again.

She handed me a basket filled with fresh sandwiches, potato chips, and cookies.

Things we could eat without heating. Things we could eat with our hands. Our dirty hands. Carefully, beautifully wrapped. So that we would have one square foot of lovely between us.

I stared at the basket. And then at her. "Carleen, this is so incredibly—" I started to say but she put her hands up and waved me to a stop.

"No, but seriously, I can't believe you did this. Thank you."

She looked at me and said, "It was nothing. It's just some sandwiches."

But it was more than just the sandwiches. And it was the sandwiches, too.

It was how *automatically* she tossed away those precious five or ten early morning moments alone on her porch with her coffee. It was the way she looked over her shoulder as she reached her door, "We'll be right there."

And it was because something in her very nature seemed to act as a sort of scaffolding for the environment around her. There were people who had so much strength that you could borrow some, just by being in the same room with them.

202

Carleen had brought more than towels and a Shop-Vac and sandwiches into our home; she had brought grace itself, carried it in her bare hands and left it there for us.

In that basket, hidden beneath one of the sandwiches and cunningly tucked right between a chocolate chip cookie and a bag of Cape Cod brand potato chips was Christmas itself. Pure, true Christmas. Unavailable at any mall or even Cartier. The hardy, incorruptible, and now exceedingly rare variety of Christmas—more of a *substance* than a holiday. Ingesting even the smallest amount would cause you to stop whatever it was you were doing and listen, listen, listen for the sound of bells high in the sky above you.

It was the night before Christmas, six days since the flood. And we'd learned a few things.

It *was* the German gay faucet.

Cheap plastic valve, aggressive tighten-happy plumber.

And nine humidifiers and industrial fans? You can't fight the noise. You must give in. You must enter it. It is the only way.

We also learned that if we had discovered the water

an hour later, we might have had to rebuild the house. Instead of just the first floor. Which we learned would consume a lot of money and most of a year to repair.

And we learned that it felt kind of nice to walk on warped floorboards in bare feet.

So.

Yeah.

Dennis came into the bedroom where I was propped against the pillows emailing my friend Haven. "Dennis seems really fine," I wrote her. "I mean, I thought he was going to be a vegetable, I thought he was going to be really sort of damaged by this. But by that evening, he was pretty much okay."

I looked up from my ThinkPad. "Hey," I said.

"Come on," he said.

My first thought was: *Oh no.*

But he was smiling.

"Come," he said, motioning with his hand.

I closed my laptop and I followed him.

We reached the bottom of the stairs and I just stared. But he took me by the hand and brought me over.

The room was dark. It was hot as hell. And loud;

that Satanic dehumidifier near the fireplace would pul-verize my mind if I had to be near it for long. And just below us in our fully wrecked non-rec room, a whole pack of dehumidifiers and fans were screaming away, as they did at every moment. I just normally didn't stand directly above them—I avoided this floor all together.

But none of this mattered.

Because there in front of me was the most beautiful Christmas tree I had ever seen.

It was perfect.

And when I saw that one of the branches was broken and in one or two spots only an ornament *hanger* was attached to the branch, then it was even more perfect.

Most of the ornaments, though, were new; I hadn't seen them before.

"When did you do this?" I asked him.

"Tonight."

"But why?"

He was silent for a moment.

Then he said, "I wanted you to have your Christmas tree."

All I could do was stand there and watch it.

Dennis watched it, too.

A couple of times, he turned to look at me and he was smiling.

And I wasn't smiling.

But then I did, a little.

And he was holding my hand and I was holding his back.

We stayed that way for a little while.

Then without us even knowing it, midnight arrived. And it became Christmas.

"I'm very lucky," I whispered, so that my voice wouldn't crack.

He squeezed my hand.

"I always have been, you know."

"I know," he said.

He bent over and picked up the extension cord near his feet. The lights were plugged into the end of it.

I assumed.

"Merry Christmas," he said, smiling at me.

He pulled the plugs apart.

And instantly, the house fell absolutely, perfectly, blessedly *silent*.